I DO, I DO, I DO
LOVE ALWAYS WINS
How God Restored our Marriage – A Personal Testimony

Patricia Gault

Kingdom
Publishers

I Do, I Do, I Do – Love Always Wins

Copyright © Patricia Gault

ISBN: 978-1-913247-07-2

1st Edition by Kingdom Publishers
Kingdom Publishers
London, UK.

DEDICATION

I would like to dedicate this book to my husband and our long-suffering children. It's been a lengthy and troubled journey... but we made it through intact. Finally, I dedicate this story – His story- to the Lord Jesus Christ, who carried each one of us through the troubled waters and has landed us victoriously in a spacious place with joy.

Contents

PART THREE

INTRODUCTION

I Do; I Do; I Do falls into the testimony book genre. It is a memoir, a powerful story of love and forgiveness in the midst of betrayal and heartache. It is written primarily from a wife's perspective. The strength of this book is the story itself of marriage restoration – all the more amazing because it is true.

This book is intended for those who find their marriages are in trouble, but who still love their spouses, and wish to find an *alternative* route to the finality of divorce ... also if divorce has already taken place – this book is for you. And this book is to give hope to those who are in despair – whether you are people of great faith, of little faith, or of no faith at all.

I DO; I DO; I DO
(Love Always Wins)

I am still confident of this: I will see the goodness of the LORD in the land of the living. Wait for the LORD. Be strong and take heart. Wait for the Lord. (Ps. 27:13-14)

These verses have been marked in my Bible over eleven times within a period of twenty years.

God's promises are worth waiting for, even when *His timetable doesn't match our own expectation or desires.* (New International Version Bible study notes; author's emphasis)

Who would have ever thought it? Who could ever have imagined when I first set eyes on James, my charming husband-to-be, that we would be repeating our marriage vows no fewer than three times over the course of 37 years? If someone had said this would be the case, I would have lashed out verbally and accused them of being totally deluded, fanciful – not switched on to reality at all...

~~

Nonetheless ...

◼◼

PART ONE

CHAPTER ONE

A FAMILY HOLIDAY

A day without laughter is a day wasted. (Charlie Chaplin)

Having made our journey by air to Finland, and then by car, then ferry and, finally, by rowing boat to our little island, we, the Gault family, were ushered around the log cabin by our host. The alluring smell of the pine wood was very evident and the crunching of the pine needles beneath our feet as we walked with our suitcases up the winding path, was a welcome contrast to the tarmac path at home; the cabin was light and airy and we started to relax at the prospect of spending the next seven nights in such pleasant surroundings. Our children, Emily who was ten and Ben, almost eight, thrilled at the sight of their bunk beds and fought over who would be in the top bunk. Next was the bathroom where there was a choice of wooden buckets and paddles on display.

But where's the all-important loo?' I asked, with a hint of alarm.

'Oh but we passed that on the way up,' said our host, almost nonchalantly; it now dawned on us that the wooden shack we had passed coming up the winding path was *it*. Later it was termed as 'the long drop'.

Our children thought this was so funny. Their imaginations were running overtime: the scenario of Mum or Dad donning wellies and hugging loo rolls, plus torch, stumbling out into the night. They had already had a laugh at my expense earlier, when my handbag suddenly slipped from my grip, albeit briefly, into the water as we transferred from the dock to the rowing boat; however, I managed quite deftly to retrieve it without any damage being done, nor loss of content.

Once we had familiarised ourselves with our new environment, it was time to explore. It was an ideal spot for the children to swim and fish and play hide-and-seek amongst the island shrubs and pine trees. James was able to unwind and relax, whilst we both caught up with vital holiday reading and generally enjoyed each other's company.

The Finnish friends who had introduced us to this idyllic place stayed in a family holiday home on another island just a few miles away. We were invited to join these people whom we hardly knew, to enjoy some 'Finnish hospitality,' at what we had understood to be 8 p.m. for a meal one evening. However, after returning to our rented car, having just tucked into a late lunch, the biggest family-size tuna fish pizza ever, there was a note on our car saying: 'Looking forward to seeing you at five o'clock.'

Well, we were given a warm reception, not only by these friends, but our nostrils were greeted with the aroma of good home cooking, which under normal circumstances would have been most welcome. A huge four-course meal had been prepared in our honour and it was being served up immediately. How we *ever* avoided each other's eyes, kept straight faces and were able to sit politely eating our way through this meal, I'll never know, but we managed somehow. Feeling uncomfortably full, we all waddled out, at our friends' suggestion, for a sauna: ladies with ladies/men with men. Fortunately, it was getting dark by this time. The tradition in Finland, following a sauna, and having slapped oneself with branches from the pine trees, was to then take a running jump into the lake, totally naked. I managed to cause a fit of giggles from the children, by sitting on a chair, only to discover pine needles sticking in my backside.

It was late August/early September. The year was 1994.

Soon our cosy little bubble was about to burst.

==

CHAPTER TWO

BAHRAIN

I am making a way in the wilderness and streams in the desert ... (Isaiah 43:19)

At the last minute we were able to get four seats on an overnight flight to Bahrain. Of course, not seated together. We were all over the place. Ben was in the back row. James, my husband, one row ahead of him. Emily nearer the front. I was in the aisle opposite her. Before the lights dimmed, I took a quick glance at our scattered family: James was knocking back a tumbler of whisky and water; Ben, with earphones on, was engrossed in a video game and Emily was trying to decide between playing Word Search or doing a crossword. I sank down heavily in my seat. My book kept slipping out of my hands as tiredness overwhelmed me.

Now, within a year of our Finnish trip, friends, working on temporary assignment in Bahrain, had suggested we join them for a short, last-minute holiday. We had known Rollo and Jen and their four children since our youngest and their second youngest were babes in arms. We had moved into their neighbourhood in the UK, when Emily was 18 months old; Ben was born whilst we lived there. They were good friends, and we were keen to see how different their lives would be on a short assignment to this far-flung and interesting part of the world. Well, according to their correspondence it sounded interesting. We were yet to find that out.

Our flight touched down at break of day. It was just after 6 a.m. We taxied across the tarmac at Bahrain International Airport, approximately five miles from the capital, Manama. There was just one sleepy terminal to greet us. Not like the award-winning 'best airport of the East' as it has now become; the old one having been pulled down and replaced by two huge bustling terminals and a magnificent hotel.

The heat outside appeared as a dubious shimmering haze. The cabin doors opened. A blast of hot air slammed into us. We descended, stepping down into an unknown environment of both ancient and modern. Were we prepared for what was ahead?

The heat was so exhausting, even at that early hour. How would we cope with it later in the day? Having retrieved our baggage, we packed ourselves into our gleaming white Honda saloon, much relieved to find air conditioning.

There might have been thoughts, but no words about James mislaying his international driver's licence in our haste to leave home. The documents were just as we left them: on the hall table by the front door. This meant that I drove the rental car. It pinged incessantly if I exceeded the 70 km speed limit. We approached the motorway ramp. It pinged. As we drove along the edge of the desert, it pinged. A pained expression registered on James's face. This wasn't driving! We were moving at an excruciating slow pace. The tension mounted in the car.

Outside the car, as I looked, this land had a beauty of its own with stark contrasts. The modern highway was interspersed with creamy white buildings and many date palms; people were living normal desert lives: busy going to market or out doing chores, before the extreme heat of the day.

Out of nowhere, we suddenly saw sand coming at us in full force. Not a gentle breeze of beach sand; this was the strong white sand of the Arabian desert. It all but obliterated our view. I slowed right down to a 'pingless' crawl. The wind whipped up desert debris blowing everywhere. The car was now covered with desert dust. Not used to these conditions, I became anxious and applied the wipers and grasped the steering wheel, desperate not to veer off-course, conscious also of my precious cargo. It wasn't long before I could see out through the windscreen again.

There had been a few gasps, but no one said a word. The dust had blown up suddenly, then, just as suddenly, all was calm.

Finally, after passing a motley bunch of camels, we reached the gated compound. The guards at the gates were there to protect those within and keep the camels out. They waved us through. As we slowly approached the house, we could see our friends sweeping sand from their porch into a mound, obviously used to these sudden sandy squalls.

Both Emily and Ben were ready to jump into their swimming pool with our friends' children to cool off. Rather foolishly I forgot to apply suntan lotion at that early hour; poor Ben paid for it with sunburn for the next couple of days.

During our stay we were driven across the hot dusty desert. A few days before we arrived there had been the very rare occurrence of flooding after heavy downpours. The desert had turned into pools in places, and the locals, who were so unaccustomed to this, would stop and jump out of their vehicles and wallow, like hippopotami at play, in the sandy water for sheer enjoyment.

We were fascinated to visit 'the Tree of Life' which is located in the middle of the desert, surrounded by miles of sand, looking all green and lush and somehow out of place. This would later become a prophetic picture of our story.

Whilst in Bahrain, we were invited to attend the confirmation service for our host's son in the local Protestant church, and there – looking as though it was straight out of Holy Trinity, Brompton, UK – was a banner advertising an Alpha Course (a course investigating the Christian faith). I believe Bahrain in those days was quite open to the gospel message, despite the majority of people being Muslims.

Foreigners were well treated, so long as they didn't venture beyond the 'safe' places. One time we found ourselves lost whilst driving and had to turn around in what looked like an unwelcoming shanty town, with menacing stares from the local folk. We were happy to be back on the main route once again.

When we were not enjoying the beach, which included some enjoyable trips out on a banana boat, we visited some interesting museums, in order to escape that midday furnace. Shopping in the souk district, buying a few local nick-knacks, was a memorable experience; the aromas in the market place varied from sweet bouquets to a tangy array of coloured spices. The atmosphere was vibrant and exotic. Many pearls, the sticky dates, the multicoloured woven materials, along with the swishing long linen garments (mostly white) worn by the men, to combat the heat – in contrast to the stark black burqas and hijabs worn by the women – all contributed to the sights, sounds and wonders of an unexpected holiday in this delightful land of palm trees and turquoise sea.

But, not unlike the sudden hot desert winds during this time, there was an unwelcome, invisible, yet tangible 'wall' which seemed to separate James and me, trying to prise us apart. The only conversations we had seemed to be punctuated with sniper-attack remarks to one another. Not only was it the heat, but tension was rising – we were both hot and irritable towards one another. Here we were in a different country and a different climate, but it seemed we had now entered into a new phase of our journey of marriage – bordering on animosity.

We were not the best of company for our hosts. At least Emily and Ben were able to enjoy their holiday with our friends' children.

The sun shining down on the hot desert sands of Bahrain would induce mirages that would play tricks with the mind's eye, and cause one to see things that just weren't there. Alas, the underlying tensions between James and me were not figments of the imagination and wishful thinking was not going to make them disappear. In my state of bewilderment about what was happening to our marriage, I started to ask myself questions about why this tension was rising between us; turning to my Christian faith for answers – but at this stage I just couldn't find any.

An inevitable storm was brewing and would very soon come to a head.

CHAPTER THREE

A BIT OF BACKGROUND

I was born in the UK in 1950 – the second child out of four children (three girls and a boy). My parents, both British, were happily married for well over 50 years, before Dad died, followed by Mum five years later.

At the age of six-and-a-half, I had an accident; I smashed into a little girl in the school playground. My two front teeth were left dangling by their nerves. An emergency dental procedure saved my teeth, but rather left its mark on me – let alone my leaving a mark on the other girl – making me very self-conscious. My teeth were glued back into my gums within a silver encasement (a la 'Jaws' in a Bond movie) which embarrassingly I had to wear for the next six months of my life – much to the amusement of my boy cousins, who would rib me over my 'dazzling grin' as the sun shone on all the silverware in my mouth. Over the next few years, and after what seemed like several hundred visits to the dentist and plenty of hardware, miracle of miracles, 'the ugly duckling finally resembled the swan she should have been' – but I was always seeking the reassurance that I was acceptable and looked OK. This resulted in rather throwing myself at the opposite sex as I grew into my teens and had many boyfriends, as I sought their approval.

Mum and Dad gave my sisters and brother and myself a secure and happy childhood, punctuated with much fun and laughter. They sacrificed a lot for us four children to have a decent education. Although I would not describe myself as academic, my strengths were in the areas of French, Art and Scripture – as well as owning a wacky sense of humour. Actors and authors, artists, vicars as well as nuns came from my father's side of the family; my happy disposition came from Mum's side. After a spell at Lucy Clayton's, I worked at Promotions for a while, then trained to become a Secretary/PA.

~~

James was born in 1949; he was the last of four children. He has an older brother and sister and another sister who passed away in 2009.

At the tender age of eight, young Jimmy was sent away to a boarding school and remained there until he was eighteen. Without doubt this experience had a profound effect on him, but as he never knew anything else with which to compare it, he accepted it and thought it a normal existence at the time. It probably did his emotional development considerable harm and might account for his subsequent reluctance to show feelings and the development of a somewhat introspective nature.

He never really felt part of the family. Being the youngest, seldom at home – and being allowed to get along on his own when he was – his parents, having had three earlier children, assumed a somewhat detached attitude to him and, as it appeared to him, they seemed to focus more of their attention on his older siblings. In fact what he really wanted was to be included in everything.

James got through school with just about acceptable exam passes and arrived at aged eighteen, not at all sure what to do with his life. He decided to emigrate to Australia during which time he worked as a trainee land surveyor, living in Perth. After two years he returned to the UK via Johannesburg in South Africa. These experiences gave him a real sense of adventure, a fondness for the outdoors, experience of being responsible for himself and an awareness of life away from the UK.

In 1974, he embarked on a career in sales and found a job working for IBM in London. While he much enjoyed life with the company, after a few months he resigned and joined a smaller IT firm and thereafter worked in an insurance brokerage.

~~

We first met at a friend's house party in Kensington on a cold and foggy night – the night that Graham Hill, the racing driver, was killed in an air crash; the year was 1975.

Apparently, James was fascinated by me. One of the advantages of writing this book is that things have been revealed which would have gone totally undiscovered and unmentioned – so it was quite a revelation, and heartwarming to hear that, on first meeting me, James described me as 'bright, funny, competent and very attractive' ... I was also 'easy to be with'.

Did I really fit such a bill?

Personally speaking, once we started settling into the humdrum ways of married life, I doubt we would have really found the opportunity to discuss those first magic moments, as we did much more recently. You can imagine the scenario after many years of marriage. At the breakfast table: 'Pass the sugar please, darling' – and 'By the way, what were your first thoughts about me when we first set eyes on each other?' It just doesn't happen that way.

Initially, I felt I would be a fool to let go of this one – there before me was this tousle-haired young fellow sporting a cheeky grin, and with the most piercing blue eyes ever. In his early twenties, just a year my senior, he was innocently handing out a tray of hors d'oeuvres. His voice, which I have always found attractive, was as someone recently described it, rich, smooth and velvety. My knees were doing the proverbial knocking and I was totally bowled over – as the expression goes. 'Where have you been all my life?' I mused. The feeling seemed mutual. Although it was like love at first sight - it was more like lust at first sight. Who can say what love is when you first set eyes on someone? It takes years to learn what the 'love' word really means. But I was hooked, and I understood that in order to keep this one interested, rightly or wrongly, I had better play at 'hard to get.' So, quite out of character, I decided rather callously to play it cool; that I would two-time him for a good few weeks after that first encounter. This was so not my usual style; my little ploy worked though. Having been snubbed a few times on a few dates, James finally called on me where I was renting a room from an aunt and uncle of mine in West London and declared his intentions towards me were serious – at which stage I waved the other chap goodbye – permanently.

For the first little while it was James, Pat and Hugo. No, not another person – but a big, black and white, spotty, slobbering dog belonging to my aunt and uncle; Hugo seemed to enjoy coming along for the ride, as if he was my personal escort. We would all squeeze into James's small whizzy sports car and spend many happy hours driving to the coast, the country or just to the local park, where we would walk and walk, talk and talk, generally getting to know each other better. I would then be dropped off in West London, whilst James spent many hours removing Hugo's copious bits of short hair from his beloved car.

After a few weeks, I had moved into a flat in north London, shared with a friend. In the end that proved to be just a temporary arrangement. As James and I became more and more involved, so we started to look for suitable rental accommodation; I knew I wanted to be married to this man, and permanently. But supposing he didn't feel the same? Was I going to regret this decision?

The day dawned when we managed to cram all our worldly chattels and belongings into James's sports car, which groaned ominously as we drove over Richmond Bridge – heading for our third-floor flat in an older building. That first evening, eager to show off my culinary skills, I made what looked like an ace Spanish omelette. Alas, all its fine ingredients went crashing to the floor, as the pan handle broke off. Perhaps supper at the local pub was the better option?

━━

CHAPTER FOUR

BIG DECISIONS

Life is a bowl of cherries. (Bob Fosse)

Within a few months of setting up home together, the sports car had been sold and replaced by a more sensible model. It was the extremely hot and muggy summer of 1976. James admitted to having driven at least three times round a roundabout before deciding whether or not to pop the big question, as by now James had apparently decided that he loved me very much. So, gingerly, over a bowl of cherries, he proposed. I didn't say 'Yes' straightaway.

In those days one could still send telegrams. I telegrammed my inglorious response to him at his place of work the following day, and it read as follows:

**HAVETHOUGHTABOUTIT*STOP*

YESWILLACCEPTYOUROFFEROF

MARRIAGE*STOP*LOVE*STOP**

So, after not too much time had passed my questions were answered. From his proposal it was now evident that James *did* want to get married. He bought me a beautiful engagement ring, which, because of its design, I called 'my diamond sandwich'. We now lived together, making plans for our future as man and wife.

CHAPTER FIVE

TYING THE KNOT

To have and to hold ... (Church of England Marriage Vows)

We had recently visited my parents and James had obviously spoken to Dad and Mum asking for my hand in marriage. Evidently his family were happy with our decision to finally tie the knot – so it was approval on all sides.

My initial introduction to James's parents was fraught with embarrassment. They lived in the west country and their son, whether it was a wise decision or not, decided to introduce his future fiancée to the local brew of cider before introducing her to his parents. I highly underestimated the strength of the drink, and after a brief 'How do you do?' to what seemed like all four of them – I struggled upstairs to sleep off the effects for a couple of hours. Was I a suitable match for their son?

So, all this leads up to the spring of 1977 when we got married - for the first time. My parents had recently moved up to the north of the country. They weren't too happy with our decision not to marry locally to them. It seemed more appropriate to get married in the church which was local to James's parents' home in the west country – the same home in which they kindly offered to hold our wedding reception. There were about sixty guests in attendance.

As we newlyweds drove down the road, waving them all goodbye, with tin cans tied on with ribbons clanging and stones rattling in the hubcaps, we stopped the car further along in a lay-by. Looking at each another and laughing nervously, we asked one another quite simultaneously: 'What on earth have we just done?' And a lot of people's stories would have ended quite happily there. But no, this was not to be ... Yet.

CHAPTER SIX

HONEYMOON AND BEYOND

FAMILY: where life begins and love never ends. (Unknown)

After a honeymoon in beautiful Greece, James and I emigrated almost immediately to Canada. We left the shores of the UK and duly set out for pastures new, heading west across the Atlantic Ocean. James had found work in Toronto with an insurance company, enabling us to get visas. I worked as a PA in a firm of architects. We lived in rented accommodation and settled down to a pleasant existence with enough money earned between us to save for a house deposit. James happened to see a job advertisement in the paper for a sales representative for a successful computer company. He was hired and we moved to Calgary, Alberta and I found work there as a PA with an oil and gas firm.

With two salaries coming in, we were able to buy our own place to live. With great excitement we watched as our new-build took shape in the south west corner of Calgary – with nothing (then) between us and the Rocky Mountain Range. There we experienced extremes of temperature: very dry cold in winter, which made for excellent powder skiing, and quite long hot dry summers. Life was good, and we made friends at work. James enjoyed his job and was quite successful. His self-esteem was rising and he was becoming more confident in himself. Whilst sitting on the doorstep of our first house in the suburbs of Calgary, we decided that after five years of marriage it was time to start a family.

~~

I became pregnant straightaway; we were ecstatic and wrote home to our families. Alas, I miscarried baby number one at eight weeks. At the time I just felt numb, and James didn't know how to console me, but we concluded that though it was not meant to be, at least we were fertile. We discovered that it is quite a common occurrence. It didn't make things any easier, but we both felt even more determined to try for another baby. Bingo – within two or three months, our second attempt was a success, and I became pregnant again when we were living in London, Ontario, having been relocated there by James' company.

At the three-month stage of my pregnancy, we were invited by friends from James's workplace to join them in renting an apartment on the island of Maui, following a business convention in Hawaii. James and I were rather suspicious of this couple, as they had mentioned in passing that they were born-again Christians. What did that mean exactly? Did they whip out their halos on high days and holidays?

Although James and I had been married in church back in the UK, that was just a formality, as everyone else seemed to do so. We had asked the vicar to bless our rings at our wedding, which he refused to do: 'Not appropriate during Lent,' was his self-righteous reply. Well, if that was what Christianity was about, we were not interested. But what did we, as a couple, think about all this 'Jesus' stuff?

~~

Questions of Belief

Faith was never discussed much at home, whilst I was growing up. Our parents gave my siblings and me a protected childhood, amongst which there was a smattering of Church of England input. But God was mainly limited to Sunday school lessons. My sisters and I, however, always prayed the Lord's Prayer every night – albeit in robotic style. Our brother portrayed the typical angelic choirboy, on the outside, but the scuffed shoes, darned trousers and catapult hidden in his cassock gave him away.

The middle school I had attended gave me a foundation of faith, with Bible stories related by a delightful, ancient Christian headteacher. The topic of Divinity always fascinated me. I was confirmed at age fourteen. I was a seeker from an early age. However, being a 'spiritual seeker' also caused me to be a bit of a rebel; as a young adult I dabbled in the things of the occult – not realising its danger until later. (More on that topic later.) My teen years were somewhat wild and without much direction. I didn't quite know what I was seeking, and became rather promiscuous – searching for 'love' in all the wrong places, which resulted in my having a very low self-esteem. You could say I was anchor-less and totally self-absorbed. Becoming a firm believer eluded me till my mid-thirties.

James' parents did not demonstrate a faith. However, his mother, by all accounts attended a Billy Graham event and was moved by it. She subsequently attended Church of England services quite regularly. His father appeared to go along with the church-going, but James never recalled the subject of faith ever being discussed at home.

Having been bundled off to boarding school at the young age of eight he would be the first to admit that his schooling also introduced him to the basics of Christianity, but it was rather marred by those in authority, who gave what's good a bad name. So he was never duly impressed with the topic. He was confirmed at age seventeen – but the process and event meant nothing to him.

~~

So, back to the tropics of Hawaii – and what I now describe to be a 'holy set-up'.

As I waded into the breathtaking blue/green/turquoise Pacific Ocean surrounded by softly swaying palm trees, miles of soft white sand, and with the sun beaming down on us, I made what I thought was quite an innocuous comment to our friends: 'Isn't life great, but why are we all here?' Not really expecting an answer to my throwaway question, I was astounded when they replied: 'Well, did you know that Jesus loves you and died for you 2,000 years ago?' What an extraordinary response to my question! What did Jesus have to do with it, I wondered? Did they really believe all that? Wasn't that namby-pamby tooth fairy stuff?

No doubt they had been praying for the right opportunity to speak about Jesus. I had just walked straight into the trap. They continued to explain the gospel message, and that history was broken in two with His timely arrival on planet earth, with the world marking its calendar from the birth of God's Son. Slowly, something was registering in my brain and later I told James:

'If this is so important, I feel cheated that no one had ever shared this information before.' He just 'herrumped', shrugging his shoulders. The topic failed to interest him and it showed.

However, it wasn't until another five or six years had passed and the births of our two children – our daughter, Emily, and son, Ben – that I personally made a conscious decision to become a Christian.

Even though the two of us had heard the same message, James was not interested at all.

~~

Our daughter was born in April 1982 which gave us a great source of pride and happiness. James discovered that being a father added a whole new dimension to his life and he felt it brought him and me closer together.

Return to the UK

In the spring of 1983, at James's request, his company relocated us back to the UK and he started work in one of their offices south west of London. We bought a house on the outskirts of a fairly large city and settled back down to life in the UK. By this time, I no longer worked full time. Fortunately, we didn't seem to have any money issues.

~~

Life went on and James had found satisfaction with his work; he enjoyed the people whom he met and the associated travel, which soon became pan-European and subsequently international.

Our son was born in October 1984, which was a huge joy and welcome addition to our little family. With a toddler and a baby to contend with, I was far too busy to think about church, but those faithful Christians who first introduced us to the faith would send me tracts telling me what becoming a Christian entailed. I would read them, and promptly hide them under a pile of nappies, out of sight, thinking, *'O well, when I am good enough*, then I'll become a Christian.'

CHAPTER SEVEN

EARLY DAYS

Will you walk into my parlour said the spider to the fly …? (Mary Howitt)

I was out walking one day, pushing a pram containing six-month-old baby Ben. Our black lab, Leo, was on the lead on one side of me, and Emily, who by this time was three years old, was on the other. Coming towards me was my mirror image; Josephine was my age. The baby boy, Tim in his pram, her daughter, Amy, on one side, plus she had a dog straining on the lead on the other. We laughed out loud and couldn't *not* acknowledge each other, and so got chatting. Emily, being Emily, immediately invited these new found friends home for 'a cuppa tea and bickies' – as was her custom.

It emerged that Josephine and her husband Pete were temporarily renting a house in the area whilst waiting for alterations to be done on a lovely old property that they had just bought, set in beautiful gardens a few miles away.

Inevitably, James, I and our children, plus Pete, Jo and theirs would spend a lot of time in each other's company. Emily and Ben had instant playmates and enjoyed the freedom of racing round the grounds of their friends' new home.

Jo and I would help each other out with childcare, if ever we had appointments to attend, or important shopping. Jo was an excellent seamstress and often made beautiful garments as presents for our children. I would feel rather inadequate as I was unable to return the favour in like manner. James and Pete seemed to get along well, too. There were fun times as the children grew up with our two families' lives being so entwined.

One summer, Jo and Pete had rented a beach hut down on the south coast – Emily and Ben were invited to spend a few nights, having great fun crabbing, swimming and playing endless games on the sandy beach. Their little lives were certainly enriched by this friendship.

Although Josephine and I got along well most of the time, I found Josephine's lack of disciplining her children a little alarming. James and I had tried to teach Emily and Ben right from wrong as we had both been taught; we didn't want either of our children to think that they could get away with rudeness and rebellion, and disciplined them accordingly. No doubt Jo found me to be a bit overbearing. And compared to Josephine's 'There, there, Sweetie' way with *our* children as well as her own, I felt that I probably appeared to her be a bit of an ogre!

Anyhow, this was generally found to be a great friendship with both families getting along famously – or *so I had thought* at the time.

CHAPTER EIGHT

LIFE'S QUESTIONS NEED ANSWERS

For God so loved the world that He sent his only Son, that whosoever believes, shall not perish, but have eternal life. (John 3:16)

In April 1986 the Chernobyl disaster happened – I was terrified at the possibility of a nuclear cloud coming to envelop the children, James and me and all our loved ones, so I wrote to our Christian friends in Canada, expressing my deepest fears. They replied that *once* you become a Christian, the peace of God gives you the security of heaven being your next destination.

'What an extraordinary reply,' I thought. 'Don't we *all* go to heaven automatically when we die? And what's all this about "becoming a Christian"? Aren't I one already? If heaven is real, then is hell *also* real?' Of course, I would do whatever it takes to avoid going *there*, if it also exists. Although their response sounded rather extreme to me, I did ponder their words ...

Not having been surrounded by people of faith as a child, I didn't yet understand the value of human life. Conversations around the 'muddled Middle East' resulted in suggestions from some family members to 'bomb the lot of them', to which there seemed to be agreement. I'd overheard someone very close to me telling a friend that she had had an abortion. Then later I discovered that another close relative had also had one. I had heard it said that if one doesn't value the Creator, then how can one value His creatures? No one had told me just *how* valuable I was as an individual. But how can anyone get *to know* the Creator? Was that possible?

I knew I was embarking upon a quest to find life's answers. I had written a little note to myself and hidden it in my handbag, asking 'someone out there' what this life was all about.

Despite having a loving husband and two beautiful children, my heart and soul felt an emptiness. I just *knew* there must be more to this existence than what I was experiencing. This dis-ease must have been in response to the continuing prayers of those faithful friends of ours in Canada.

CHAPTER NINE

PLUNGE

O taste and see that the Lord is good. (Psalm 34:8)

By now our little family had moved from the outskirts and into the city; we bought an older house set within spacious gardens, in which to bring up our children. Emily and Ben attended a small church school, where they received a more rounded view of Christianity than either of us had received.

In the November of 1987 an Australian evangelist called John Chapman advertised that he would be holding meetings in the local city's town hall for five nights. Like a moth to light, I *knew* I had to be there. It was, no doubt, those faithful praying friends again – and I told James so; it resulted in my going on three of the five nights. On the last evening the evangelist talked of Jesus calming the storm and speaking to the wind and the waves, and I thought, 'There's something about this Jesus I've got to try and understand, but what? And how?' It was then that the evangelist talked of some people 'sitting on the fence' about their faith, and it's *not* a comfortable place to be. I knew he was talking straight at me, or that's how it seemed.

When he asked whether anyone felt they wanted to become a Christian, I was the first one down to the front to respond for prayer. Nothing – nothing or no one was going to stop me.

Later, at home, my husband just could not fathom quite what had happened to his wife that evening; he felt powerless to even try. Meanwhile, I was flying high on a completely different planet; or that's how it seemed. I had just become a brand new Christian: I had been born-again. In hindsight, it would have benefited me and everyone, had I been packed off to a desert island with my Bible, before ever speaking to anyone about my faith. Alas, 20/20 vision was not evident in my case.

I became rather obnoxious to all those around me: in my enthusiasm and pride, all I wanted to talk about was this new-found relationship with Jesus. I was disobedient to God's Word (the Bible) to wives about adopting a *quiet and humble spirit* – 'winning your husbands over, without even saying a word' (1 Peter 3). I had so much pride, that the very word 'humility' got stuck in my throat. I would talk faith all the time. This unfortunately became a major sticking point in our marriage – something I would bitterly regret later, of course, and wish I had paid more attention to the wise words in the Bible.

James was patient with me – at first. He believed this was just a phase that I'd get over. I had come to understand the importance of the gospel message, and I would be used to tell older people – several terminally ill males, some even on their deathbeds – about how they might receive God's love, salvation and forgiveness through his Son, Jesus Christ. And though I found it such a privilege, all the while the gulf was widening between James and me. Even the poor window cleaner would be subjected to my evangelistic efforts. I would stand at the bottom of the ladder telling him the Good News, with him at the top mopping our windows, listening. He eventually became a Christian. I discovered this fact after an elder at my church told me that he had received a phone call from an Irish window cleaner informing him of his decision.

Friends of mine who saw me at a distance would cross over to the other side of the street to avoid speaking to me: 'Oh no, it's that crazy born-again woman.' But within two years they had all become Christians.

James got both barrels – we still loved one another, but tensions began to arise and the rot started to set in, and when it was evident that he and I no longer saw eye to eye on various issues, he started to resent the time I would spend going to church or church-related events. Would he have been happier had I taken up drinking, smoking or loose living?

Initially he did join me and the children on a Sunday, but that waned after a while. It wasn't that he denied seeing positive changes in his wife; there were a number: from the start I was put off the taste of strong alcohol; I stopped using God's name in vain; my dress became more modest; and answers to prayer were becoming undeniable. James admitted to feeling as if his wife was having an affair with this invisible Jesus, but he couldn't 'bop him one on the nose'. Unfortunately, I couldn't see it this way (then), and instead of zipping my lips I would spout forth a-plenty.

Bit by bit James became angry, not only with my ramblings, but that my faith was something beyond his control.

~~

We spent a holiday that summer in Norfolk. I took a lot of teasing and leg-pulling for my faith from both James and his sister – with whom we'd gone to stay. But that was manageable as it was done quite amicably and there was no offence taken on my part. It was an insight as to what Jesus meant when he said in Luke 4:24 that 'A prophet is not honoured in his own town', and in John 16:33 that 'In this world you will have trouble. But take heart! I have overcome the world.'

Nonetheless, as time progressed and our marriage became more of a challenge, I needed to quote this often to myself – which served to remind me of those opposing views we both had.

⚏

CHAPTER TEN

POWER FROM ON HIGH

But the Holy Spirit will come on you and give you power ... (Acts 1:8)

After hearing a sermon on the topic of baptism in the Holy Spirit, I asked the curate at the church I attended to pray for me to receive this gift. He placed his hands on my head and prayed; I received a heavenly language – the gift of tongues. At home, when alone, I would practise speaking in tongues – even singing in it. One day, whilst singing in the kitchen, I found both the dog and the cat sitting there with their heads cocked first to one side, and then to the other, listening intently – it was as if they knew this was something supernatural happening.

During those early days I spent praying, I was given many messages and promises, and was instructed to write them down. One in particular went along these lines: *satan* (the evil one) *wants to sift you like wheat – you must be prepared to go through times of sifting, for your faith is being tested. My plans will come about in ways that you cannot think or imagine; you are to stay calm and be willing to do My will. Be able to tell others that this is the Lord's will – for I am going to do great things in your lives. Be able to hold your head up and declare My praise at all times!"*

Also: *At the right time I will pull all things together and make that imperfect balance perfect. Consider not the ways of the world.*

There were also warnings that: *You will be purified by the fire – to be used at a time of My choice. Walk humbly with your God. Trust only in Me, for I will not let you down.*

Well, in between the nice and encouraging words, there were some *not*-so-nice and encouraging ones – quite scary ones in fact. As a new Christian, I was so overwhelmed with the almost unthinkable idea that the God of the universe was conversing with *me*, that, at times, I was sceptical. I had no idea what all this meant – but felt up to the challenge, and kept a journal with all the 'words' I received.

My faith was growing day by day and I knew and accepted that the Lord was going to have to do a lot of work on me, personally, to prepare me for whatever was up ahead. 'Bring it on, Lord,' was my reaction. Unfortunately, I wasn't considering how my decisions, words and actions were affecting my husband, for the most part negatively. How differently things *could* have worked out, had I been more obedient to God's word, and more sensitive to James's feelings, instead of being so wrapped up in my faith. I did not realise then just how much this would cost me in the future.

I got into deep water one time whilst at a supper party at non-Christian friend's house. There were about eight of us round the table; we were just settling into our desserts – the men were discussing business matters, and us ladies – well, the topic of our conversation was 'nits' (head lice). The other mums were lamenting the fact they couldn't find *anything* effective to eliminate these little critters from invading their children's heads of hair.

'Well, try telling them to "Go, in the name of Jesus" – and *they will*,' I piped up.

Suddenly the room fell silent. All eyes were quizzically upon me – then upon James. 'Time to go,' he mouthed to me. We made our excuses and a swift exit, and drove home with a big black cloud hanging over us both.

'... And *why* did you have to bring up *that* topic just this evening?' he said angrily. I had just offended him big time as far as he was concerned. It had now become so second-nature to say these things as my Christian friends and I had seen such great results, that I had not taken into account any respect for my husband's feelings, and had unwittingly put him in an embarrassing position. Why had I been so blind and uncaring? Like the Apostle Paul (from Romans 7:15), I said to myself: 'I do not understand what I do. For what I want to do I do not do, but what I hate I do.'

I asked forgiveness from both James and God. I needed God's wisdom to read and obey Proverbs 31:12: 'Wives, do your husbands good and not harm all the days of your lives.'

==

CHAPTER ELEVEN

MY SHEEP

Speak, Lord, for your servant is listening. (1 Samuel 3:9)

At a Christmas service held at a nearby cathedral, I 'heard' the following promise, which I claimed for myself: 'Blessed is she who has believed that what the Lord has said to her will be accomplished.'

The reader has every right to ask why this woman believes she hears from God. It was after I had received baptism of the Holy Spirit that this happened; coupled with the verse from John 10: 4-5: 'My sheep know my voice.'

In my daily Bible-reading time, I would sit with pen and notebook and just listen expectantly. I sometimes tried speaking God's promises back to him: 'He is my Good Shepherd' and 'His sheep hear his voice', and a quote from the boy Samuel (from 1 Samuel 3:9): 'Speak, Lord, for your servant is listening.'

I then found to my utter amazement that words and sentences formed within my own thoughts that I knew didn't or couldn't have originated with me. If I doubted where they came from, I would declare under my breath: 'Jesus is Lord.'

All the while I was developing this relationship with him, I would spend much time worshipping him, and literally basking in this new-found state of *extreme* love. It felt as though I was walking in a dream – an enchanting dream known only to me. No doubt, as other Christians would testify, this honeymoon period doesn't last forever. There comes a time of testing and pruning. In the Bible it says one's faith is of more value than gold or silver (1 Peter 1:7), and he puts all of us believers into situations that test and strengthen us. We sometimes need the harshness of the north wind to blow upon us, tempered with the soft south wind; all of this is necessary for character building, in order for the bearing of much fruit for God's Kingdom. This generally results in the encouragement of other believers, plus many more people being added to the Kingdom of God.

This 'divine love' encounter in no way diminished my love for my earthly mate – my husband James. But it was becoming something which, regrettably, I could not share with him. And he, it seemed, was also unwilling to receive. But over time, and totally unaware of what was beginning to happen, both our hearts towards one another were becoming cold and hardened...

~~

Becoming a Christian did have its amusing moments. Once, whilst hanging out the washing, the phone rang and it was my mother – as if to test me, she said: 'Well, your uncle D needs a miracle – I've just bumped into him on the way from the dentist. Apparently he had gone for his normal early-morning dip in the sea, and has lost his top set of false teeth, but his dentist is away – he mumbled in a gummy way, baring only his bottom teeth – so, you will have to pray one of your special prayers to God...' I laughed, and went back to hanging out the washing.

'OK, Lord, over to You, only You can re-unite my uncle D with his teeth. Thank You. Amen,' was my simple prayer. Later on that evening, Mum rang back and said: 'You'll never guess what happened!'

I waited expectantly.

'Your uncle D went out for his early-evening swim, and what should be floating in the water on the incoming tide straight ahead of him?... only his false teeth!'

I praised God for this miracle, and His sense of humour. It also indicated to me that my mum must have had the beginnings of a seed of faith to call and ask me to pray, which proved to be very reassuring for me, as she had originally been very sceptical about my faith.

More seriously though, at an Easter service at the church I attended, the amazing truth of what Easter meant hit home to me very hard – I was bowled over by what Jesus had done for me and for the whole world. I wept out loud when I realised the seriousness of my sin – having lived so selfishly without ever really having acknowledged him in my life before, plus all the other shameful things I'd done/said/thought or not done, and of which I was not proud – compared to His total selflessness, pouring out His life's blood for me and for all mankind.

Every day, as I read my Bible and prayed to know Him better, my life was gradually being transformed by the Lord's loving guidance. I found my confidence, value and identity was in Him. This didn't, however, score many brownie points within my marriage. There were times when James would lash out verbally – and once, in his frustration when we were asleep in bed, I felt a clasped fist smash down on the pillow next to my head – missing me by millimetres. This happened in his sleep. It needs to be added that James has *never* been violent with me.

A member of the prayer group I attended was given quite a graphic 'picture' by the Lord, of James resisting the wooing of the Holy Spirit to become a Christian: 'he was inside the nozzle of a gun, hanging on to the sides for dear mercy – resisting God with all his might. God's hand was on the trigger.'

CHAPTER TWELVE

WATER BAPTISM

Accept what is; let go of what was and have faith in what will be.
(Sonia Ricotti)

Having been christened as a baby, I determinedly dismissed the idea of being baptised as an adult – after rather cruelly mocking a friend who had also been baptised as a baby, but who was now electing to be 'fully dunked'. She wisely suggested that I come before the Lord and ask him if and why I should be baptised. This happened within five years of my conversion. I did so, and it was the first time I had ever heard the Lord's voice speak to me so clearly! It was the most humbling experience and I made a note of our conversation:

Patricia: *Lord, how can I put right what I've done wrong for so long in my life before knowing you?*

Lord: *You can't. Only I can, and have through Jesus' death.*

Then the Lord showed me Jesus' life and ugly, painful physical death on the Cross, followed by a worse, far worse, spiritual death, down in the bowels of hell – Jesus being attacked by all the wild dogs of Bashan – being ripped and torn apart, taking upon Himself what should have been *my* punishment.

Patricia: *Lord, show me the significance of total immersion baptism.*

The Lord showed me Jesus being baptised in the River Jordan, going down and coming up out of the water with the Spirit as a dove upon Him – God's voice saying, 'This is my beloved Son, in Him I am well pleased' – then Jesus said, 'I can do nothing on my own, I only do what the Father tells me to do.'

Patricia: *But Lord, didn't my old self die to sin when I became a new creation at* *my conversion?*

The Lord showed me a new butterfly emerging from its shed cocoon – then He showed me the necessity of the total cleansing by water. You leave all the shed cocoon and its connotations down in the water, so it disappears down the plughole, gone for ever – washed clean away – to emerge a brand new, publicly declared person in Christ.

Patricia: *Lord, where would you have this take place?*

Lord: *At the church of your choice. This is your day. You are doing this for me not your husband. He will come – he loves you so, he sees your devotion to me – he will come and witness your baptism – though he might not necessarily choose that place for himself.*

Patricia: *Shall I tell James about this and show him this communication?*

Lord: *Leave it with me – I am working in this man's heart and mind. Don't you worry. You have a mighty man of God here in the making. He will do great things for me.*

Together, you will do great things for me. [what awesome promises!]

So, I had no choice but to be baptised; I felt that I needed permission from the Church of England church I had previously been attending – and was met with a stern: 'No – that is not the way we do things here if you've already been baptized as a baby.'

'Well, it was at the Lord's suggestion.' They couldn't argue with that one. He is, after all the highest authority. So I went ahead and got fully dunked wilfully. It was an amazing, unforgettable experience. It happened just as it was meant to, with all my sinful past disappearing down the plughole – and me emerging up out of the water feeling like a brand new, clean person, totally cleansed from *all* my sins. It was a very liberating and uplifting experience. And yes, James did come and witness it, along with both of our children, but I could only detect confusion in his facial expression. He looked uncomfortable and detached from the event.

CHAPTER THIRTEEN

POPPIES

Parable of the Poppies

One day, whilst walking the family dog, I asked the Lord to speak to me from nature. He suggested that I might go and study the poppies growing at the edge of the field. As I did so, I was seeing them in all different stages of growth, and picked up one of each stage, thinking:

'Wow, this is *so* like my walk with the Lord.'

The First One was all green with its head hanging down – representing me before I became a Christian, no real joy, and blinded by all the wrong things I had done.

The Second One was mostly green, but the cap was almost off, revealing the redness of the poppy within. This represented the time when I heard the Good News of the gospel, but I hadn't yet asked for God's forgiveness, nor yielded myself to Him – so the cap of 'sin' had not yet been removed.

The Third One was all red, but all wrinkly. This was the stage of being a brand new Christian, with lots of issues yet to be sorted out/ironed out.

The Fourth One, and what I thought was the final one, as there were many of these, was all red and smooth, just enjoying the sun/Son-shine – depicting my walk with the Lord up to that point..

I was overjoyed with this amazing lesson, thanking the Lord. I continued on my walk – but He called me back to look for one more!

There dotted sparsely amongst the vast array of open red poppies, were one or two with a very black centre to them, in the form of a cross!

My heart skipped a beat, as I felt the Holy Spirit whisper to my heart: *'And this is how I want to be – enthroned on your heart for ever in indelible black ink, living for me, serving me and loving me because of what I've done FOR YOU on the Cross at Calvary.'*

'Thank you, Lord Jesus. You are absolutely amazing! Let it be unto me as your words say.'

Little did I know then just what that would mean later on.

I grabbed a handful of each of these poppies in their various stages, and made a quick visit to my Bible group leader – keen to share with her my latest lesson in life, before they withered.

Much, much later, and on a different walk with a different dog this time – I came across yet *another* poppy. This time I must have audibly gasped. There was the bright red poppy, with the black cross at the centre, but behind the cross was brilliant white – depicting the joy and victory of Christ's resurrection brilliance and victory.

A friend of mine was inspired to write a poem in response to my experience:

My Friend, the Poppies & Jesus

My friend went walking one morning
In a field of poppies so red
To take her dog for a run in the field
When a whisper came into her head
'Look at the poppies my daughter, look at them well' the voice said.

She gazed down upon the wonderful sight
Poppies so warm and so red.

Her eyes stayed on one drooping flower
Another one caught her gaze
This one was slightly lifted
And the next had a head gently raised
A joyful and wonderful sight
And just in the midst of this poppy
A beautiful cross came to light.

She looked at the one all crumpled
And quickly went down the rest
Picking the one with the wonderful cross
Remembered how much we'd been blessed.

We are all like these beautiful poppies
We start off with heads bowed down
Till the Lord makes us grow with his wonderful love
And we end with his beautiful crown.

So we must obey when we hear that small voice
And the wind blows the Spirit of power
To hear and obey as my friend did
The blessing that came in a flower.

(Diane Green, 1994)

CHAPTER FOURTEEN

RESCUED

The Lord rescued me from my powerful enemies, from those who hated me and were too strong for me. (Psalm 18:17)

Earlier, I mentioned my previous involvement with the realm of darkness, before becoming a Christian. As well as being an avid follower of astrology – believing in the star signs – I had had my tarot cards read, but even more seriously, I had also taken part in séances as a teenager.

I didn't know all this was something which I needed to renounce after my conversion to Christianity. I did not realise I was headed for a satanic attack.

James was away on a business trip and you could say I was vulnerable and still very young and inexperienced in my faith walk. It started with me wishing to have the interpretation of tongues and, as I was praying, this deep unknown voice started to speak within me. Literally, I was being taunted by a spirit of deception – the manifestation of which resulted in the constant sensation of having my head and neck being pushed forward. I was somehow of the belief that the Lord would use me in a *spectacular* way to bring healing to my mum – the 'voice' had told me she was terminally ill [in reality, she wasn't] – plus salvation to family members who needed it. These lies, coupled with a suggested fast from food for a week, caused alarm bells to ring in the mind of my local Bible group leader, meeting at our house. She expressed her concerns to the then curate of the church we both attended.

Was it more than a coincidence that he had just attended a conference on 'Spiritual Warfare?' He questioned my previous pre-Christian life, and upon learning of my occult involvement, suggested that I might renounce these evil practices – stating very sensibly that:

'One cannot walk into a swamp without picking up leeches.'

So immediately, I did as he suggested and renounced my involvement in the occult – not wishing to be taunted any longer; plus I wanted to obey the Lord, and it was suggested once more that I pray 'the sinner's prayer' – meaning that I acknowledged my sin and asked for God's forgiveness.

The Lord also caused a friend to drop by, as she had been given the words from 1 John 5:5: 'Who is it that overcomes the world? [i.e 'the world, the flesh and the devil'] Only the one who believes that Jesus *is* the Son of God' (italics added).

Whenever I quoted that vital verse, my head and neck would lift up once more back to normal. It helped to get me through a very difficult time.

After the prayers of the curate and our Christian friends – who *happened* to be visiting from Canada, I was set free permanently and delivered from this wicked taunting spirit at last. It was a wonderful comfort for me to have those original Christian friends who witnessed their own faith to me all those years before, there in our own home to pray with me and support me.

This exercise served to show me that the devil is real and powerful, but God's power through the shed blood of Jesus is *far* greater, and that the Lord has given us authority over *all* the works of the evil one. It also demonstrated the great importance of renouncing any and *every* previous involvement with the enemy's rightly owned territory. Being a legalist, the enemy will fight his corner, where necessary. By my own sin of delving into his territory, I had given him legal ownership, hence my need to renounce it all.

Upon James' return from his trip he found a slimmer and slightly paler wife. It was God's providence that the two of us were booked to go on a cruise to Baja California the following week, whilst good friends were taking care of Emily and Ben. I was able to enjoy the food and recuperate in the sunshine, and try to explain to James – in words that he could understand – exactly what had happened to his wife during very that testing week.

~~

Upon first becoming a Christian, I was told that I had not joined a cruise-ship – more like a battleship. I was also advised to put on the 'whole armour of God' (from Ephesians 6:10 onwards), which I did daily.

It wasn't till recently that I thought I was becoming rather legalistic following this pattern of praying. One night I had a dream: I saw myself as a weak pussy-cat putting on this armour daily, but the Lord told me that the devil doesn't see us like that. Instead he sees a fierce roaring lion (as in Jesus, the Lion of Judah) and the devil trembles with fear.

==

CHAPTER FIFTEEN

A CHILD'S FAITH

Train a child up in the way he should go and when he is old he will not depart from it. (Proverbs 22:6)

Our two children – Emily and Ben – independently became Christians at the ages of seven and four respectively; both were filled with the Holy Spirit and spoke in tongues. One of them even received the gift of interpreting my heavenly language. We would experience wonderful times of worship, Bible reading and prayers after bath time or before bed time. Many prayers were answered for friends and family and for the family pets.

On the ferry coming back from France one time when the children were quite young, the kids and I were singing a worship song. Suddenly the Holy Spirit broke through, and the three of us were singing in tongues – it was like the angels in heaven were joining in ... James couldn't help but be visibly moved by it.

It seemed everything our daughter Emily prayed for just seemed to 'happen.' When quite small, she prayed very specifically for a Wendy-house: 'Please Lord, could it be white with a red door, and a green roof – Oh yes, and with criss-cross [lattice] windows? Thank you – Amen.'

She knew just what she wanted – though she'd never before seen one. Well, within the week, her prayer was answered. Someone was selling one *with that exact description*. It was paid for and delivered immediately – a very loved Wendy-house. She thanked the Lord.

So many answers to prayer whilst growing up encouraged her to pray to the Lord to provide a mattress for her bed at uni. He did – a beautiful one, which had hardly been used, for just £50.

Another time, as a student, her hair had become rather matted and unkempt, part of which resembled a dreadlock – though her usually lush and long hair was cleverly hidden under a headscarf. 'Mum, I can't stand these dreads any longer – I miss having my normal hair – will you please pray that the Lord does something.'

Well there was *no way* one could even get a brush or comb through – so I took her to the hairdresser who said: 'The only thing to do would be to cut it all off and grow it again.'

'No way,' groaned Emily, bursting into tears.

But before doing anything as drastic as that – and as a kind gesture – she did suggest a different conditioner. That evening as we washed and applied the conditioner, with comb in hand, I was poised at the ready: 'Well dear Lord, you parted the Red Sea – so this head of hair is no problem to you at all.' And amazingly the comb went through her hair so smoothly; there was only one small knotted area, hidden at the back, to which I took a pair of scissors – but the next day, she had her beautiful long locks back – much to everyone's wonderment, especially the hairdresser's.

Once again, thanks be to God. These are but a scant handful of examples.

There were also healing miracles. The children both prayed for James after he had tripped down a curb and had badly twisted his ankle – the swelling went down, and it was healed straightaway. Ben, our son, seemed to get more than his fair share of childhood ailments, but after praying he would soon be restored to good health once more. He was told at 8 years old that he would become a 'leader of God's people' when he is older. Watch this space.

Ben often received 'pictures' from the Lord – he saw the Lord Jesus in heaven sporting a white robe with a blue sash on it saying 'Saviour'. He described seeing a beautiful rainbow and saw that the road to heaven was white and narrow; however, there was a thick dark road to hell.

I recorded in a book all the words, 'pictures' and dreams our children received from the Lord.

CHAPTER SIXTEEN

JAMES: 'I NEED A CRISIS'

Don't judge my path if you haven't walked my journey. (Unknown)

By this time, James recognised a feeling of unreality relating to work and his own existence. He was beginning to think that his success and failures, in business, were not down to him or his individual efforts at all, but a result of the brand for which he was working. Additionally, as mentioned, he was frequently angry at home and lashed out at me and the children. In summing it up, he felt that working for a big corporation with all its peer pressure to perform, the internal procedures for salary and performance reviews, made him feel insecure. He was at the beck and call of his superiors and his self-esteem and confidence levels were directly related to his relationship with them. Being somewhat diffident just heightened the feeling.

This 'unreality' resulted in his feeling that he was on a treadmill from which he could not get off. He felt that he was a bit of a fraud, just basking in the success his company was having, rather than feeling that he, personally, was successful. He did not feel authentic or in control of his life. He could not conceive leaving the company, as he felt too insecure to believe that outside of his company environment he would do anything else but fail miserably, so he had no alternative but to remain and suffer all those feelings.

It could be said that his public school experience had left him without a true sense of self, one that was secure in the knowledge of who he really was, as opposed to being a version of himself that he felt was acceptable to others. Basically, in order to get out of this loop he felt that he 'needed a crisis'.

●●

51

PART TWO

CHAPTER SEVENTEEN

PARTIAL ENLIGHTENMENT

God is like oxygen – you can't see him, but you can't live without him. (Unknown)

Away on holiday in France one summer, when the children were still young, James awoke in the middle of the night having had a dream. He sat bolt upright and declared: 'There is a kingdom of darkness and there's a kingdom of light, and they are clashing.'

'Yes,' I agreed sleepily. 'That's very biblical,' – and then went back to sleep.

At the time, I was interpreting it as a general state of our lives as Christians – but I didn't realise then that it had all become a personal clashing of the two opposing kingdoms within our own marriage.

Another time, as I was clearing out the children's toy cupboard, I found a handwritten letter written by James. It was a very humble note written as to the Lord, asking him to change him and to fill him with the Holy Spirit, as he had witnessed what He'd done in my life and the lives of others we knew. If I had not seen that it was James's own handwriting, I would *never* have guessed it even came from him, because by this stage his temperament was becoming angrier – and I had become quite fearful of it. He was mocking my faith and was frustrated with life in general. I wept as I read the letter (as it was undated, I had no knowledge of when exactly it was written).

I kept quiet – for once – and hid it away. Months went by during which time the fortunes of the company where James was working had waned; a redundancy programme was initiated and James opted for voluntary redundancy. One morning, whilst having a cup of tea in bed, James, said to me: 'I wish I had your faith.'

'Well, I believe you do –- in a certain measure,' was my response.

'What makes you so sure?' he asked. At which stage I showed him the letter. James was not at all happy that I had found it – thinking that he'd successfully binned it. I felt sure I was *meant* to find it to remind me later just where my husband stood with his own faith-walk.

There were times when I was also instructed to *'journal things on a daily basis'*. At that stage, I had written that James, having just read the first six chapters of St John's Gospel, awoke one morning at 3 a.m. and said to me: 'My world is being turned upside down.' And after completing the whole Gospel he just announced: 'Boy – if this stuff is really true, there's going to be *no stopping me.*'

But ...

~~

James, as noted previously, is one of four siblings, as am I. Two of his siblings divorced, as have two of mine. Almost like 'babes in the wood' James and I entered into marriage thinking that our love for each other would be enough to fend off any ravaging wolves.

We were wrong.

The battle was about to begin.

CHAPTER EIGHTEEN

STRANGE PROMISES

Happily ever after is not a fairytale – it's a choice. It's a decision to love, forgive, grow and grow old together. (Fawn Weaver)

James and I had been married for almost 20 years – it was ten years into this marriage that I became a Christian. On our 19th wedding anniversary, I felt the Spirit of the Lord whisper:

'You and your husband will grow old together.' I wondered why he gave me such comforting and reassuring words at that particular time? But I was so glad he did – as it was something to which I could refer, and on which I would depend time and time again later on. Only the omnipotent, omniscient and omnipresent Lord knew what was to take place in our lives during the next fifteen years or so.

I found that the Lord gave me these 'pegs' around which I could wind my rope to steady myself as I ventured upon this journey up life's mountain. These 'Rhema' words (God's Word revealed) were ones to which I could fasten my trust and hope and he proved to be so kind as he prepared me for the battles ahead. He is *so* utterly dependable and faithful in this walk or climb called 'life'.

I have always been encouraged by the Lord to keep believing; keep looking forward; to not listen to the voice of satan who would try to put me down, bring condemnation or just tell lies. Many were the 'words' which involved James' and our future together.

I was a bit put out one day when a friend from church gave me some 'words' she had from Job 13:15 which read: *'Though He slay me, yet will I hope in Him.'* And Job 23:10: *'But He knows the way that I take; when He has tested me, I will come forth as gold.'* Did I rejoice, or tremble at these words? What would you have done?

==

CHAPTER NINETEEN

THE BATTLE BEGINS

You might have to fight a battle more than once to win it. (Margaret Thatcher)

I had *not* consciously done anything to reverse the gradual disintegration of James and my marriage relationship – details of which have already been mentioned. I felt that we were hurtling along on a train, whose tracks were never ending, and that we were not going to stop either.

Rather selfishly I had not considered my husband's feelings enough about my dramatic faith conversion. He must have felt vastly outnumbered by his direct family members – with both Emily and Ben now embracing a faith of their own, let alone the feelings of rejection and isolation. Only in hindsight did I realise that this could have triggered similar emotions to those of being sent off to boarding school at that tender young age.

Also, I had not done myself any favours by approaching my parents-in-law and James' siblings with my tireless enthusiasm for Jesus, with me not wishing that 'any should perish' – through their seeming lack of knowledge of the way of salvation. Alas, my well-intended approach seemed to fall on deaf ears.

Although I was not to know what shape or form it was to take, the previously warned-of 'sifting' started within our marriage.

~~

A huge bombshell was dropped when James suddenly gave me the ultimatum: 'It's God, or me.'

==

CHAPTER TWENTY

FIRST AFFAIR

... for better or for worse ... (Church of England Marriage Vows)

The bottom dropped out of my heart – this was a *devastating* ultimatum – I loved my husband. I couldn't become un-born again, *so I chose* to trust God for this marriage, not quite realising at the time what that might mean. We stumbled on for a while.

It Got Worse

James had joined a smaller company a few months after taking his redundancy; however, this proved to be a stopgap, as nine months into the job he received an offer from another more suitable firm. He joined in March 1995, and as well as quickly resuming relationships with well-known customers, he started travelling again. It was during one of these trips to foreign soil that he met a woman whom, he later admitted, for some reason he found attractive, and felt somehow that this relationship 'was real and authentic' and appeared to give him greater satisfaction and relevance to that which he was finding with me. James also found that he could excuse himself on the basis that he could not fathom or live with my Christian commitment. As my ears heard, and my eyes saw him mouth these words, a million things just seem to be exploding in my head, as I tried to take on board the enormity of this shocking and unexpected news.

After he had returned from this particular business trip, I *had* sensed a change in James's attitude. He was never one to get emotional over the films we watched, but during one particular film – *Father of the Bride*, with Steve Martin – I noticed there were tears in his eyes, and it wasn't a particularly 'weepy' film. His attitude towards me had also changed. For instance, before his trip we had together chosen an attractive decorative flower arrangement to be made up – which James wished to give me. But when he returned from his trip and we went to collect said piece, all interest or enthusiasm was completely missing from him. I couldn't believe the contrast in his attitude. It seems he couldn't have cared less, and it not only surprised me but it stung too.

I found myself in complete denial at first – I dared not think the unthinkable. Finally, I plucked up the courage to confront him. My world was shattered when the one I had loved and trusted the most in the world, now admitted his unfaithfulness to me and wanted out: 'I've met someone else and I don't love you anymore.' (These were actually lies from the devil, but I didn't realise it at the time.) Ouch – *double ouch*.

This news stunned me to the point where, if I didn't have skin all around me to keep me all in, I felt that all the fragments that seemed to have come loose would have spilled out there and then. My mind went into 'shattered vase' mode – I even momentarily forgot *all* the words and promises that I felt I had previously received from the Lord.

I moved into the spare bedroom. I telephoned one of James's sisters to inform her. Upon our engagement, she had initially told me that I'd married a 'solid rock' – and I needn't worry about him 'messing about'. But her response this time was: 'Why has your faith become so all-consuming, Patricia, almost to the exclusion of James?' I had no satisfactory answer to give her.

Our future suddenly began to look all too bleak.

After the initial shock, I went before the Lord. My first reaction was immediately to relate to how the Lord must have felt when he was betrayed by his friend, Judas Iscariot. It was comforting to me knowing that the Lord *knew* exactly how I was feeling.

Once the dust had settled, however, my following reactions were not quite so saintly and loving – I'm a human being after all, and we *hurt*. There I was, planning all sorts of nasty things to take my revenge: I was positively spitting venom. I had read somewhere about a woman cutting off every left trouser-leg from her unfaithful husband's business suits hanging in the wardrobe, putting sugar in his petrol tank, and afterwards arranging for a mountain of manure to be delivered to his new address. These menacing thoughts somehow became appealing to me – then I thought better of it.

James and I decided not to inform Emily and Ben just yet, because no immediate plans had been made. The kids must have sensed the ill-ease between us and our heated discussions and disagreements would have added to the already tense atmosphere. So we all limped along – a family falling apart at the seams.

CHAPTER TWENTY-ONE

FORGIVE?

*And when you stand praying, if you hold anything against anyone, forgive them,
so that your Father in heaven may forgive you your sins.* (Mark 11:25)

I saw a lady whom I'd previously known; she was walking down the road looking very sad. I caught up with her and asked why she looked so troubled – she informed her that her daughter had been murdered and, understandably she felt so angry and upset with her daughter's killer that she felt she wanted to go and strangle him. How terrible for this poor woman.

Not having been in the position then of having to forgive anyone myself at that stage, I rather piously suggested she read the parable of the Unforgiving Servant in the New Testament (Matthew 18:21-35).

It's about the servant who owed the king millions of pounds, being unable to pay his debt back; begged for mercy, only to have the king forgive his debts and cancel them – the same servant then met a fellow-servant who owed *him* money, but declined to show him any mercy when he begged him for more time, and threatened him with jail, till he could pay him back.

Other servants heard this tale, and reported it back to the king, who called back the original servant and demanded why he didn't show mercy to his fellow-servant, as he'd previously asked for mercy for himself, which had been granted – and the king had this wicked servant thrown into jail, until his debt was paid. It seemed I was trying to give this lady a formula for forgiveness ...

But now, the shoe was on the other foot – *my foot*. It was now me who had to find it in myself to do the forgiving – I was also a Christian – a *new creation*, and I now had choices.

CHAPTER TWENTY-TWO

FORGIVENESS

Forgive us our sins as we forgive ... (Matthew 6:12)

At the time of James' confessions, I ran a bath and just soaked in it for hours thinking about the Lord's Prayer – 'Forgive us our sins, as we forgive those who sin against us.'

'Oh Lord, this is so hard, but I do choose *to be willing* to forgive James – and the other woman – as you have forgiven *me* so much in the past,' I prayed.

I felt something the moment I made the choice to forgive. I knew it was the moment when healing began to come into my broken heart. It was so releasing – so freeing. I have had continually to choose to forgive ever since. Do many people realise what a vital key forgiveness is to their healing and wholeness? I prayed my friend would find it in her heart to forgive her daughter's killer.

There was a tug of war going on in James's heart; the enemy muscled his way in somewhere to bring temptation, because of satan's loathing for anything the Lord has instituted – whether it be the Church, or marriage. In Ephesians 5:21-33, Paul compares the relationship of husband and wife to that between Christ and His Church. This makes marriage an obvious target for the devil; if he can destroy marriages, then he can destroy generations of marriages.

Notwithstanding my own contribution to the dastardly outcome of things – and I confess to *my part* in the breakdown of this marriage, as a result of thinking that I knew better than God! When I was first converted and was so 'on fire for Jesus' I thought I could 'save the world before breakfast', including my husband. I soon discovered that God is bigger than all my aspirations. As you know already, I disobeyed all the Scriptures that pointed to such wisdom, which at the time I foolishly chose to ignore. I had a lot to learn, and I learned the hard way – attending the

'University of Hard Knocks'. Maybe someone reading this might be saved a lot of heartache, just by choosing to be more obedient – and thereby avoid being sent to the same 'university'.

James packed his belongings and left us on the approach to Christmas 1995.

CHAPTER TWENTY-THREE

GOING, GOING ...

Faith doesn't always mean that God changes your situation. Sometimes it means he changes you. (Steven Furtick)

Presents had been carefully wrapped and placed up in the cupboard away from prying eyes, and pesky pets. The Christmas tree which had been beautifully decorated by Emily and Ben, *not* without a squabble – was placed in its usual spot in the living room. The fragrance of the orange and cinnamon decorations the children and I had made earlier on permeated the air, and it all added to the magical *Christmassy* atmosphere. Baby Jesus was safely in his manger, having been rescued from the jaws of Buzz, our recently acquired pup.

The telephone rang: 'Hello Mrs G – your tickets are ready to be collected.' It was the travel agents.

'Oh – were we going somewhere?' I wondered, putting the phone down. I went upstairs to inform and question James. He was packing a suitcase.

'Are, err, are we going somewhere?' I asked him tentatively. He shifted awkwardly.

No; it turned out that we – that is the children and I – weren't going anywhere, but *James* was going somewhere to be with 'someone else'.

At this point we still had not mentioned anything to the children. As James and I came down the stairs, the children were coming up – they suspected that 'all was not well'. How right they were. We all met together on the landing. The scene made a strange little cameo.

It was time to inform Emily and Ben of what was *really* going on.

'I hate to be the one to announce this to you, darlings, but your father has decided to leave us,' I was forced to say, sounding very mechanical. It was a very tense moment.

In the midst of tears and the heartache of divided loyalties, our daughter, aged 14, declared loudly: 'I *want* to go and live with *you*, Daddy.' (Alas, this was impracticable.)

Our son (then aged eleven) announced: 'Mum, even if we have to live in a tent, I'm staying with *you*.'

This more or less embodied the children's attitudes after James left: Ben remained loyal and supportive, whilst Emily, though sympathetic up to a point – deep down felt I deserved to have her dad leave and found it hard to forgive me – although I didn't fully appreciate this fact until a few years later when Emily went away to university.

Of course it was hard for Ben and Emily to understand *then*, given their young ages, as they didn't have a clue as to the bigger picture –which I was still trying to grapple with myself.

~~

Without further ado, James upped and left. I managed to press into his hand a copy of *that letter* he had written to the Lord.

The memory of that day became a hazy blur, but one thing I do recall was that, that evening, we were at least united in our prayers to God to help this broken family. Every night Emily and Ben asked God to change their dad's mind, heal the rift and bring him back home.

CHAPTER TWENTY-FOUR

FIRST CHRISTMAS ALONE

God speaks in the language you know best ... not through your ears, but through your circumstances. (Oswald Chambers)

Each morning when I awoke to the empty space on his side of the bed, my innards would twist and groan – I just couldn't grasp the reality of what was happening. Though I felt wretched and, over time, dropped two dress sizes, I knew that falling into a 'pity party' was not the answer, plus I wanted to try, with God's help, to keep the atmosphere at home as normal as possible – no ranting or blaming, just getting on with life.

My parents came to stay with the children and me over Christmas for a few days. James had already written to them explaining his reasons for leaving. Though they still loved me, they were not exactly empathetic towards me – still not fully understanding my spiritual conversion – but were still very supportive, as were all my family. At their departure, I was facing New Year's Eve all alone. I prayed so much for help. My day's Bible reading was the passage 'Go out into the highways and byways and invite the people in for a feast; go call the cripple, the lame, the poor ...' I knew the Lord wanted me to open my house for a New Year's Eve party, and so I sent the invitations out.

We lived on the edge of a needy council estate – I had no idea how many would accept, and equally had no idea of how much food to prepare or buy in. I decided to just trust Jesus. I bought a moderate amount of food (pasta and sauces, salads etc.); some friends brought cakes and desserts. My guests started to arrive by about 7 p.m. – some people in wheelchairs were ushered in – there was a lot of chatter and sense of excitement in anticipation of another new year – it helped me keep my mind off other horrible things which had been going on in my life.

In the end, within a 6-hour period, there were no fewer than 58 people who came through my front door, and the food never ran out. People even came back for second helpings, yet it never diminished – it *multiplied*! The Lord was showing me that He was the God of the impossible – wow.

The icing on the cake was that one dear soul gave her life to Jesus right there in my sitting room.

~~

That winter turned out to be very harsh – it was cold and bleak. The long dark shadows of the watery sun upon the trees eerily mirrored the darkness I was experiencing. As I looked out at the trees, denuded of their foliage – this depicted just how I was feeling. I had at least had prior warning of the pruning process – but I didn't realise how hard it would feel in reality.

It never seemed right to blame God for any of this – James and I were both experiencing the consequences of our own personal choices and decisions. But God was the only one who could get us both out of this unholy mess. A song on the Christian radio station seemed to echo my sentiments precisely. I cried a lot.

~~

'The Love-Nest'

It was a cruel blow to discover that James had arranged for 'Linda' – this new woman in his life – to come and live in the UK. They were renting a property which belonged to one of James's relatives. This seemed all wrong to me. How dare he bring in this usurper and set her up in their own little love-nest.

How Ben and Emily felt with this arrangement, I could not guess.

Still, all the while, I knew I had to make a choice – would I get all chewed up inside and lose my peace or should my attitude be to forgive and to keep on forgiving? Once again, albeit reluctantly – I asked the Lord to help me forgive the pair of them, as I would be the only one to suffer if I didn't forgive.

CHAPTER TWENTY-FIVE

GOD'S CHALLENGE

It takes more courage to be humble than it does to be prideful. (Matthew Hagee)

There was a Christian article I found myself reading, about a lady who was going through precisely the same thing I was. She had even prayed to the Lord, that if she could be given the opportunity to speak to the other woman, she would tell her about her forgiveness for her (the other woman), and would state her belief that her husband would be returning to her. As I read this article, I felt courage and faith rise up in me and even prayed the exact same prayer.

No sooner had I done so, than I was challenged by God to see if I meant business. A newly made friend of mine was about to have a baby. I had written her telephone number on a piece of paper by the phone. The children had also written a telephone number on a piece of paper by the phone. It was the number of the place where their dad and Linda were staying.

Unbeknown to me – but known of course to the Lord – I had dialled this number and asked the strange female voice at the end of the phone whether my friend was there, and whether she had had her baby yet.

'Baby? There's no baby here,' came a strong foreign accent.

I suddenly realised my error – took a deep breath, sent up a very quick prayer, and announced who I was, and then said to her: 'I have nothing against you, Linda, but I do believe that my husband is coming home to me.'

You could imagine the scenario – her looking bewildered at the phone: 'Ehh? What?' was her reply. 'Who is this?'

'Yes, you heard right,' was mine.

Then I repeated the message, trembling very much at this stage, and put the phone down, not knowing whether to laugh or cry.

~~

Although determined to try and sort out my life the way I had wanted it to go, I realised that it was time for me to lay down all *my* own hopes and dreams as to how I had expected my life and our marriage to pan out – so I literally surrendered them all to the Lord, giving Him all my fears and insecurities. I even gave Him back all those words and promises He had made to me.

'Not my will but yours be done in my life, Lord.'

It sounds very pious admitting to all of the above, but I often tried clawing it all back, only to surrender again.

CHAPTER TWENTY-SIX

STANDING

Be sure you put your feet in the right place then stand firm. (Abraham Lincoln)

From the beginning, after my husband left for the first time – I felt the Lord say to *'make a stand for your marriage,'* and, through a trusted Christian friend, He gave the following: *'Like a partial eclipse of the sun – after enjoying the light for a while, your husband has 'chosen' to go into the darkness for a time.'*

Just how long is 'a time', Lord? I enquired. To which there was no response.

~~

So, I began what can only be described as a sometimes lonely and harrowing, but often exhilarating and glorious, journey – with the Lord as 'my husband'. Weekends were the biggest challenge. Walking down the pedestrian precinct in my town, seeing other loving couples, would be like a further twisting of a knife inside me, although it had been a long time since James and I were a loving couple – but I would call on the Lord for help, and I would receive the strange but reassuring sense of His presence beside me. I discovered things about the Lord that I could never have discovered, had life gone on as before – in what had now become a totally 'dead' marriage with James. Like a multi-faceted diamond, the Lord's character has so many wonderful traits. I had memorised some of the Lord's names. Some of which were:

Elohim – Creator God

El Shaddai – God Almighty of blessings

Adonai – the same yesterday, today and forever, revealed in Christ Jesus

Jehovah Jireh – Provider

Jehovah Rophe – Healer: the One who turns a bitter experience into a sweet one

Jehovah Makadesh – Sanctifier

Jehovah Nisi – Banner of Love

Jehovah Rohi – Good Shepherd

Jehovah Tsidskenu – Righteousness

Jehovah Shalom – Prince of Peace

Jehovah Shammah – the God who is always there and who will never leave us nor forsake us

And the list goes on...

It was during that 'wilderness' time of my life, that all these names describing our awesome God became a reality to me. Although it comes in different guises – my experience being unique to me – this temporary season of pruning is the norm for most Christians embarking upon this amazing journey called 'faith'. I needed to get to know better, the One in whom I had put my trust. I felt I was undergoing a crash course in this.

I knew I had to live as if I was still married – that is, to continue to wear my wedding ring; I didn't go out as a 'single'. Nonetheless, I felt that the Lord needed me to help Him to bring James back. I was operating as a 'fleshly' Christian – not realising this was all part of the bigger plan of the Lord, to enable me to become a Christian who operated in 'the Spirit'. A friend of mine was given a 'picture' of me – initially as a tall tower, but gradually having all my bricks removed. Then the Lord was in a position to build me up – brick by brick – *His way.*

This dove-tailed with another prophetic 'picture' given to me of my house, having all its walls removed for a time; the ceiling, floor and windows were just floating in mid air.

━━

CHAPTER TWENTY-SEVEN

MAN'S PLAN VERSUS GOD'S

If we wait until we're ready, we'll be waiting for the rest of our lives.
(Lemony Snicket)

There's the story in Genesis 15–16 about God giving Abraham and Sarah – then called Abram and Sarai – the promise of a son, Isaac, who would be born by Sarai's own flesh, despite their ancient and infertile bodies. However, as the years progressed, with no sign of the promised baby, they decided to 'do it their way': Sarai unwisely suggested her husband should sleep with her maidservant in order to try to fulfil God's promise. That liaison resulted in the birth of Ishmael, who although loved by God, was *not* God's promised son to them. However, within another few years, God came through faithfully when Abraham and Sarah finally gave birth to Isaac – the promised heir. It's all about waiting on God's perfect timing.

~~

You could say that James and I, as a couple, had several 'Ishmael' experiences.

==

CHAPTER TWENTY-EIGHT

FIRST ISHMAEL

The sweetness of love is shortlived, but the pain endures. (Thomas Malory)

Within some months of James cohabiting with Linda, I woke up one morning with a Greek expression going through my head. In my pre-marriage days, I had lived in Athens for a while – at the same time as the Turkish invasion of Cyprus in 1973. Exiled President Karamanlis was asked to return to a troubled Greece. The roads up to the centre of Athens were lined with people shouting out '*Ere Hete! Ere Hete!*' (He is returning). These same words were buzzing through my head – and, what do you know, my husband walked through our front door, bringing with him the few possessions he'd taken; he had come back to live once more with his family! The children and I were ecstatic, and we all took up where we'd left off.

Linda had apparently packed her bags, bought a plane ticket and had returned to her home abroad. I learned afterwards that she had written letters to both James's sisters telling them in no uncertain terms what she thought of their brother. I could have told her some things too.

Praise God – James had returned – but, after a futile attempt at reconciliation, I knew I hadn't really changed, and it seemed that neither had he.

We started attending painful sessions with 'Relate' off and on for about nine months – a total disaster. The charity is well-meaning, but it seemed to us that, as an organisation which was supposed to *help* marriages in trouble, in our case it was merely there to make way for the inevitable break-up. All James could talk about was his feelings for the other party – it just rubbed salt in my very raw wounds. Equally, he was giving me confused messages, saying that he *still* loved me. You could see he was being torn apart emotionally. But I knew that James had already made up his mind to leave us again. But before he did ...

━━

CHAPTER TWENTY-NINE

PARABLE OF THE FREEZER

Slow Thaw

One day – it was a half-term holiday – I finally got around to defrosting the freezer: life still had to go on. It was one of those chest types, chock full of food still; some out of date; some still edible – but there was an awful lot of ice which had furred up the sides. After unplugging it, I threw out the junk, and gave away some still-edible food to a neighbour with lots of kids. I finally got down to the bottom of the cavernous interior and discovered to my horror, amongst the coffee granules and loose frozen peas, no fewer than 43 twizzle tags, and 19 pegs. As I looked down into my freezer, it seems I heard a voice from God: *'This looks a bit like your marriage, doesn't it?'*

Yes, I knew this was the Lord giving me a parable I could understand – the undealt-with issues: ignoring things when they weren't right; the ice that had built up on the inside of James's heart and mine.

I burst into tears and continued trying to de-frost this thing quickly. A tool from the tool box was too severe and would have ruined the inside. I tried throwing boiling water in – only to have it ice up even more quickly. Then I heard the same voice: *'Slow thaw.'*

As our daughter came into the room and saw her mum looking like a panda, with smudged eyes, she asked: 'What's wrong, Mum?'

All I could blurt out was: 'Oh my darling, when you have grown up and have your own household and you get one of these appliances, make sure you read and obey the maker's instructions.' She thought I had truly 'lost it'.

━━

CHAPTER THIRTY

THE HORRID 'D' WORD

One of the hardest things you will ever do my dear, is to grieve the loss of a person who is still alive. (Jeanette Walls)

So, James left again – and this time requested a divorce. This horrible experience took place in 1997-8. Because there needed to be some sort of financial arrangement, I made the mistake of agreeing to it – not taking too seriously the words of God from Malachi chapter 2, which says *'I hate divorce.'* I have since repented to the Lord for treating His word lightly.

I felt the 'D' word was brandished on my forehead in flashing neon lights – it's an ugly feeling, bringing shame and confusion. Being divorced – for me, at least – was like being discarded and thrown away on the world's rubbish heap and, for a time, I felt utterly unworthy, unloved and truly wretched. I really questioned whether I had heard the Lord correctly about our marriage.

I felt I could neither *'hold my head up high'* nor did I *'sing God's praises'* – at least not at that time. But amazingly, it didn't cause me to ever lose my faith. I knew that I knew that I was loved by God. The worst thing was, I was still in love with my husband, James – and it seemed all wrong that I was losing him. I had to release him into God's hands, along with all my hopes, dreams and longings for our lives together.

~~

Like Gulliver of *Gulliver's Travels*, I felt like my hair, hands and feet had all been bound down with ropes attached to pegs and on each of the pegs was written a word: Abandonment, Rejection, Bitterness, Fear, Unforgiveness – as that was just how I was feeling. But, as I meditated on the Cross, I sensed a spiritual pair of scissors snipping me free of all these negative labels. With each snip the Lord replaced them with His positives; Acceptance, Love, Joy, Peace, Forgiveness.

~~

God didn't just leave me in a raw painful state, He came alongside me and provided a wonderful and permanent way out. Although the facts are written as they were, I have now *no recollection* of the pain I experienced then. It was at this stage that I would describe myself like that 'Tree of Life' in Bahrain. Spiritually speaking, my leaves were green and flourishing despite living in what was, naturally speaking, more like a very dry desert.

~~

When the removal men came to pack up our belongings, everything having been so cruelly 'divided up'; naturally speaking there's nothing nice about divorce, and, naturally speaking, I said goodbye to our lovely family dining table, but in faith, I said: 'I'll see you again one day' (which we *did*, thanks be to God).

It was a time of such sweet sorrow. My heart was so torn in two. Every night I would go to bed listening to Graham Kendrick's song 'All I once held dear', until the cassette wore out.

The words of the song went along the lines, that all the things in the world I was once fighting for, seem to pale into significance after finding this true relationship of love and acceptance with the Lord, rather than following a set of rules called 'religion'. It slowly dawned on me that in order to be mended and be set free, I had to come to the end of myself. It might sound bizarre to some, but I felt the Lord literally holding my hand in His, as I went fitfully off to sleep.

Passages from Isaiah 54 became very poignant to me:

verse 5: 'For your Maker is your husband … the Holy One of Israel …

verse 6: 'The LORD will call you back as if you were a wife deserted and distressed in spirit –a wife who married young, only to be rejected,' says your God.

verse 10: 'Though the mountains be shaken and the hills be removed,

yet my unfailing love for you will not be shaken

nor my covenant of peace be removed,' says the LORD, who has compassion on you.

As my mountains were being shaken, and the hills were being removed, I was able to feast upon these comforting words, and also to witness God's unfailing love and His covenant of peace and, above all, His *faithfulness*.

'Man' About the House

Where previously James would have done the task – holding up the axe to cut logs, I would call on the Lord for help – and 'Bingo', perfectly split logs. Turning the mattress of our bed, I would ask for help – and got it, without hurting my back. If I couldn't untangle my necklaces (James was a very patient man with attention to detail), I would call on the Lord and just leave them till morning in their tangled-up state. Next morning, I awoke to find them perfectly separated, several times. This didn't make my husband redundant, but God promises to be there in our time of need – He is indeed a faithful God. Amazing. He turns a bitter experience into a sweet one and gives us 'beauty for ashes' (Isaiah 61:3).

PART THREE

CHAPTER THIRTY-ONE

IN THE NICK

I will walk by faith even if I cannot see. (2 Corinthians 5:7)

So there I was, with our son and one very unhappy daughter – and understandably so, having been the 'apple of her daddy's eye'. This shock in Emily's young life caused her to become quite reckless and unpredictable. You could say she fell in with a bad crowd. One day I received a call from the local police station asking me to come down as: 'We have your daughter in a cell – she's been caught shop lifting.'

I telephoned James, who was abroad again at this time, and relayed the message I had just received – there wasn't anything he could do from overseas, so it was left up to me to deal with.

My Bible reading that morning from Isaiah 43:2 said, 'When you go through the waters, you will not drown, and when you go through the fire, you will not be burned,' so, having an incredible peace within, I 'cast all my cares on the Lord' and trusted Him for the outcome. But, when I saw our daughter there – all alone and looking very vulnerable – my heart just went out to her. I told her it was going to be alright. Emily, being repentant of what she had done, decided to go the honesty route, admitted the petty theft and would return the items – unlike the 'friends' with whom she'd been caught.

The wise officer on the case told her: 'It's quite cool to shoplift, isn't it? But, it's *not cool* to be caught.' She got off lightly with just a caution, and she promised me that would be the last time she would *ever* do such a thing. I believed her – it had frightened our daughter very much. I just knew that the Lord was in it all – but it was still a very sobering episode for us both.

CHAPTER THIRTY-TWO

FRIENDS

Good friends are like snowflakes – all different and all beautiful. (Unknown)

At the very beginning of this journey, the Lord brought me a lovely prayer partner who was also 'standing' for her marriage after thirty years with her husband. When we first met – at a prayer meeting – before we had properly spoken, this new friend suddenly piped up with: 'It's going to be alright, you know' – which turned out to be very prophetic words.

We would meet up to pray in the most unlikely of places and for any length of time, for our mates to come back to their senses, and for God to do a work in each of us. We experienced many ups and downs during our times of sharing and praying – but the Lord strengthened and protected that friendship, because the Bible says that the Lord has no favourites – He is no respecter of persons and what He does for one, He will surely do for others. We were there to encourage one another in our 'marriage stands', as it's a tough world out there: family and friends think we are crackers most of the time, but you can't blame them for not having the same revelation about 'standing' for our marriages. We found that the common thread in their comments or suggestions to us was to tell us to 'Get on with your life – forget your spouse and move on to the next person or future spouse.'

Unfortunately, we and other 'standers' all found this attitude also pervaded many of the churches we attended. However, the pastor of the free church I had moved to, *did* understand, for which I was extremely grateful. Just as a sick body needs tender loving care along with prayers to be healed up – so often does a 'failing marriage' need that sort of attention and much prayer and patience.

Mutual friends of James and me found this a difficult situation, but generally remained supportive, and with all the comings and goings, they kindly reserved their judgements.

Other 'Standers'

The Lord, I felt, had sent a 'plain-clothed angel' to my church to inform me of a group of people 'standing for their marriages' in London. This group was called 'Beulah' (which means 'married'). So God added many more dear 'stander' friends along the way, and we would often meet up to encourage one another. Not many words were needed, as each *just knew* what the other had been through. We found ourselves developing deep and trusting relationships amongst each other; we would meet up to pray regularly for our prodigals and to encourage one another. There was also a lot of online help, in the form of Rejoice Marriage Ministries (Pompano Beach, Florida) and another in North Carolina, USA, an organisation called 'Covenant Keepers'; both ministries would send biblically based help through daily emails and regular newsletters and updates of any restored marriages. Even as this is being written, these have encouragingly and rapidly been on the increase. These opened up a whole new vista of worldwide 'standers' – and it made me realise just how precious the institution of marriage is to the Lord Himself, who affirmed it in the first place.

The head of one of these ministries came to London to encourage the 'standers' in the UK. At that time there was a strapline on all British Telecom (BT) vans saying 'hundreds are returning every day' –- meaning that their customers who had gone elsewhere were returning, but for each of those waiting for their spouses to 'come to their senses' this was indeed a timely and prophetic word of encouragement for us all. The following is a quote from a fellow-'stander': 'In this world we move in today, we are the outcasts because we are trusting Him for something that is beyond our families' comprehension, our friends, and even our own minds – but that does not take away from His word and who *He* is through all of this.'

==

CHAPTER THIRTY-THREE

A NEW HOUSE

The home should be the treasure chest of living. (Le Corbusier)

The divorce went through and our pleasant family home was duly sold, much to my chagrin. Here we were saying goodbye to the house and garden where we'd jointly bought up our still quite young children. So many fond memories had been made there, and now someone else was about to embark on making their own memories in *our* house. The fun we had had entertaining friends and family; the miraculous provision of the Wendy-house – it was all so very sad. However, a lovely Christian 'army wife' friend, who'd had to move umpteen times in her life, managed to convince me that it was only 'bricks and mortar' The children and I moved into a much smaller place, which I call a 'miracle house from the Lord'.

Before our break-up, but whilst I was on my own, I attended my first Christian conference' – it was a 'Prophetic Conference' held for a few days in Scotland. I saw this as an opportunity to stay with our old friends Josephine and Pete, who had moved to Scotland a couple of years earlier.

At the end of the week, the group I was in was asked to 'prophesy' to one another – and a lovely young lad of about eighteen prophesied over me. In effect he told me that the Lord had prepared a place for me (and the children): 'It's like a cottage, but not old. There are overhanging trees and there's a little archway with roses, and a winding pathway to the front door.'

Not fully understanding or believing all of this, I politely thanked him and came home back to my life in southern England. It was only after the divorce and house sale that a friend of mine suggested I write down in a prayer letter to the Lord what I would specifically like in the new house I was about to search for.

I gave the Lord my list: 'Dear Lord, you know my needs even before I do, but I would dearly love a house with the following: at least three bedrooms; two rooms for living and eating; a cat-flap; a garden – all well maintained. Thank you. Amen.'

And for good measure I threw in a *garage* – though rare at the price I could afford. Well, how *great* is the Lord! After a few no-goes, one of the estate agents informed me of a place and had just sent details to me in the post. I asked if I could go and see it then and there. I arrived and went in through the back entrance. I began to feel all tingly, and thought, 'Well, this must be something special!' I then came round to the front and there I could plainly see – 'It's like a cottage, but not old. There are overhanging trees, and there's a little archway with roses, and a winding pathway to the front door.'

So I knew immediately that this was 'the one' that had been prepared for me and our children and that had been prophesied a year before. The Lord is so good – He continued to turn a bitter experience into a sweet one. This house ticked all the boxes; of course there was a garage as well. The first few weeks there were so precious to me, and the Lord's presence so strongly felt, I could almost see the indentation in the sofa cushions where He'd been sitting – *no kidding*.

For the first few days after our move, I found I didn't even have to cook a meal. There were people – some I didn't even know – who had so kindly cooked and brought meals to the house. I felt the Lord's tangible presence in that house. It was almost as if He was saying to me:

'You chose me – so this is a taster of my faithfulness.' Awesome.

We lived there for eight years, and although I was 'on my own' I never felt alone. It was in a great neighbourhood, with very supportive friends and neighbours all around us.

◥◣

CHAPTER THIRTY-FOUR

ROBINS

Sometimes the smallest things take up the most room in your heart.
(Winnie the Pooh)

The garden of the house from the Lord had thick foliage all around. At the back door off the kitchen, in summer, I would hear the tick, tick, tick of the baby robins which hatched from their nests in the foliage. They became so tame it was not unusual for a robin to hop into our kitchen. One sunny weekend, James, (now my 'ex'), had come to collect the children to take them to visit him (as well as Linda, who had come back on the scene once James and my divorce was through). James arrived on his own whilst we were having breakfast out on the patio. I invited him to join us for coffee and croissants and, much to my surprise, he accepted.

There we were – the whole family seated together – and then to our amazement a little robin hopped up on to the table to join us. I wished right then and there that I could have pressed the 'pause' button – it was a truly magical moment for us all. I felt this represented the Lord's presence with us – it was so special. The robin has been a special reminder of the Lord's closeness and faithfulness to me for all these years.

If ever I have needed confirmation of an important decision, 'my fleece'[1] would always be me requesting the sighting of a robin – and the Lord has always obliged.

Living Life as a 'Singleton'

So, I 'got on with my life', so to speak, but was still 'standing for my marriage'. I would tell anyone who would listen that I believed that one day the Lord would bring my husband home to us permanently and there is power in one's words (Proverbs 18:21: 'The tongue has the power of life and death, and those who love it will eat its fruit').

---

1 Taken from the story of Gideon in the Old Testament (Judges 6). Gideon asks God for a sign that he is with him, helping to rescue Israel; Gideon puts a fleece of wool on the ground and if there is dew on the fleece and dry on the ground, and vice versa, Gideon knows that God will rescue him.

I missed my husband's voice – even if we only spoke on the phone about the children, the car or finances, my heart would skip a beat to hear his voice once more.

My younger sister and her husband, who lived in the north of England, always included me, and often Emily and Ben – if they weren't with their father – on their holidays abroad. Later on, our widowed mother would join us as well, so I never missed out on times of refreshing, travelling and sunshine. I was very blessed.

When Emily reached her eighteenth birthday (and my half-century), the two of us celebrated by visiting Canada to show Emily the place of her birth, followed by a trip to Chicago, paying a quick visit to my eldest sister, who at that time lived there so that Emily could get to know two of her boy cousins – then finally ended up in New York, doing the art gallery and museums, as well as the excellent shopping that the fascinating city had to offer. It was a whistle-stop tour, but great fun nonetheless. Later on, it just so happened that James took Ben on a similar trip when he reached his eighteenth birthday, taking the train down from Canada to the east coast of the USA, but omitting the New York shops.

━━

CHAPTER THIRTY-FIVE

WHOSE AGENDA?

A single thread of hope is stronger than all the chains that bind you. (Jeffrey Fry)

It wasn't long before a friend suggested I go out for a drink with a male friend of hers who had been recently bereaved. As I felt rather sorry for the chap, I willingly agreed to go along just for 'an innocent drink' – without consulting the Lord. Wrong decision! The next day, as I came before the Lord in my quiet time, I *felt* something like chains around my ankles and in my mind's eye I looked down and *saw* the chains.

I felt the Lord say: *'Last night was not on my agenda for you.'*

'Oops, I'm *so* sorry, Lord. Please forgive me,' came my reply.

As a result I realised just *how seriously* the Lord took 'my stand' for marriage – for it was *His* stand too.

This was where my stand for marriage really began to take a new turn. The Lord had my attention now and I learned all about marriage as a covenant – not just as a contract. Whilst a contract is legally binding – an agreement between parties – a covenant is a spiritual agreement; it's a pledge. In a covenant, the party not getting their needs met supports the failing party so that they can meet their obligations.

I discovered that even if one of the spouses walks out of a relationship, they would still be viewed as 'one flesh' in the courts of heaven. Also, if just one of the spouses (i.e. the Christian) dares to believe that 'He who is in one's marriage covenant, is greater than he who is in the world' (i.e. the evil one), then a stand for one's marriage takes on a whole new meaning: it was being backed up by God the Father, God the Son and God the Holy Spirit, and a whole host of heaven's armies....

God *so* hates divorce, as His word in the Old Testament book of Malachi says. It was *then* that I realised just how important marriage is to God, and the realisation of it all empowered me. The Lord God was there alongside me and my children, to support and encourage me. This was such a revelation to me!

CHAPTER THIRTY-SIX

MY AGENDA?

Life can catch you off guard. It smacks you in the face when you least expect it.
(Joann Buchanan)

During that same year, the children came back from one of their regular visits with their dad and Linda only to inform me of their impending 'marriage'.

Shock, horror. This took me completely by surprise. I gulped hard, and hid myself away in the garden, mug of tea in hand, conversing with the Lord. I said: 'I thought you wanted me to stand for my marriage – this news is not on *my* agenda.' To which came the reply: *'This sickness is not unto death.'*

Well *that* didn't make much sense to me – I thought I must have either heard wrongly or made it up. However, in order to boost my confidence, the Lord caused another Christian friend to ring me later on that day and give me the exact same message the Lord had originally given me – and that encouraged me enormously. Upon thinking it through and locating its whereabouts in the Bible –from the story of Lazarus (John 11:4) – I realised that 'this sickness'–this 'legalised adultery'– would *not* end in death; it wasn't going to be permanent. The rest of the verse said: 'No, it is for God's glory so that God's Son may be glorified through it.'

Once I knew this was the case, I had peace for a while – it was after all in God's capable hands.

However, I was still reeling a bit – torn between wanting to believe and wanting to react in my fleshy senses; there's always a battle going on inside. I was feeling quite justified about writing a stinking hate-letter to James, just to let him know how *I* felt, upon his return from their honeymoon. I wrote the note, then slept on it. My Bible reading the next morning was from Matthew 6: 'Love your enemies, pray for those who hurt you'... Grrrr!

I then heard the Lord whisper: *'Why not send flowers instead?'* So I did – ripping up the ill-intended note, meantime.

By *God's* grace alone was I truly able to forgive and keep on forgiving – what was it Jesus told Peter? To forgive not 'seven times, but up to seventy times seven' (Matthew 18:22). In his strength *only* is it possible.

One Saturday morning, much later on, I woke up and said to the Lord: 'I feel ready to meet James's new wife.'

That day there was a knock on the door and there was James: 'Err – I was just wondering whether you would like to meet my new wife?'

'Linda – meet Patricia. Patricia – this is Linda.'

There in *my house*, I – his one-flesh wife – was entertaining James's 'wife', and somehow, again, in God's strength, I was able to remain congenial and hospitable, and neither spit at her nor tear my claws into her face. God must be changing me, as there would be no telling just what the *old* Patricia would have done. It was a complete act of the grace of God.

Our daughter and son couldn't quite get their minds around it. Much later – after one of James's and my 'false starts', James recalled that Linda was so amazed and touched by this 'act of kindness'; she admitted no one had ever been that way to her whilst she had moved to this country. Such irony. But isn't the Lord so good to prepare me and use me that way? I could not boast in myself (after all, I was ready to put that 'hate mail' into the post!). No, it was *His* work all the way.

~~

Because the house we were living in was especially hand-picked by the Lord, even both our children eventually felt comfortable there and made many new friends, and both attended secondary school and college. We spent some happy times there and, despite everything, both children came through their education with excellent grades and both achieved brilliant university degrees; this I felt, had absolutely nothing to do with me. The Lord was an excellent Father and Teacher to them: thanks be to God. He gives us a joy that no man can take away.

Isaiah 59:19b says: '... When the enemy shall come in like a flood, the Spirit of the LORD shall lift up a standard [or a banner] against him.' God's love was like a canopy over us – the children and I felt very safe and protected during those eight years.

CHAPTER THIRTY-SEVEN

SECOND ISHMAEL

All roads out of hell lead home. (Shannon L. Alder)

As predicted, James's marriage to Linda *did* only last a short time – two and a half years. In James's words it was 'pretty much a disaster from the outset' and left him in a very insecure place. He and Linda had been living in south west London and he was acutely aware that during this time he had neglected the needs of our children. To remedy this he arranged to move back to the city where the children and I were living.

On that day, I received a phone call at work from James asking me to come to where he was living and to pick him up and drive him 'home'. This phone call put me into a complete spin. James had to make several phone calls as I was driving the car – one being to the insurance company, telling them to insure the car in his *wife's* name, meaning *me*! I felt utter joy in my heart to hear these actual words being spoken by my husband – well, 'ex' at the time. Though welcoming, I remained on my guard at James's sudden return.

He had rented a flat, from which he was now running his own recruitment business. The combination of his second separation and divorce, and managing the cash flow of a recruitment company, nearly destroyed him. This arrangement lasted for about a year and things were looking amazingly positive. Because this happened as it did, I was not surprised – and rather naively thought: 'This is it – he's coming back home to us permanently.'

Whoops – I had spoken too soon.

That year went by and James was attending a local evangelical church which was holding an Alpha Course – a course aimed at investigating the Christian faith – though he didn't see it right through to the vital Holy Spirit day. He actually dropped out of both church and the course after a couple of months. He was not ready for either. I thought I had 'a right' to start preaching at him and would stomp around his flat trying to ram the gospel down his throat. So you see, I still hadn't changed in some areas.

In a spirit of repentance, I had to come and ask for forgiveness from the Lord and ask for a teachable spirit as I got back into the word of God for more learning.

Heartbreak Again

Whilst he was back in my home town, there was talk of James and me getting back together. He, however, did not feel that it was right at the time. James informed me: 'I've had enough of this Christianity thing – it doesn't work for me.'

He must have felt overwhelmed and in a state of confusion, as he promptly upped and left – and went far away into the arms of *another*. Again, I pressed a copy of the letter he had written to the Lord into his hand.

This sudden departure of James prompted another set of roller-coaster emotions which were keenly felt by Emily, Ben and, of course, myself. We were left speechless and numbed.

It was Christmas time again – just when the world is focused on the birth of our Saviour, the evil one chooses that particular time to carry out his wicked schemes. But, bless her – my sister, who lives up north and is also a Christian, felt prompted by the Lord to buy in extra food for their Christmas meals – not understanding why. When the children and I unexpectedly headed north she had three extra guests – it then all made sense.

As we sat in traffic, I asked the Lord: 'Where are you in all of this, Lord?'

Then, as I became aware of the traffic being stationary – we were in the middle lane – I looked to my left, and a huge truck's strap-line was 'We Remove Your Mountains'. Then to my right was a smaller truck sporting the name 'Shepherd & Son'. I giggled.

'Oh that's *so* encouraging! Thank you, Lord.'

Peace reigned once more.

~~

The first time around this mountain I found it was almost a doddle to forgive my husband and *his* now 'ex-wife'. The Lord gave me so much grace that I almost felt sorry for Linda, as I knew that it wasn't going to last ...

~~

All in all, given the previously mentioned circumstances and resulting emotions, James was not in a good place and fell prey to the advances of a divorcée, with whom he had a relationship (off and on) for the next four years. However, this divorcée – James's new paramour – just *happened* to be none other than Josephine, my old 'best friend' from way back when. Would you believe it?

CHAPTER THIRTY-EIGHT

SECOND AFFAIR

Never, never, never give up. (Winston Churchill)

It was Emily and Ben who broke the news to me that Josephine was 'the new *other* woman'. I nearly passed out when I heard. Now it was even more painful knowing that my children would have to experience divided loyalties towards their dad and Josephine – because they knew just how I would receive the news. They also admitted finding it difficult seeing their dad treat Josephine in a way they had not seen him fittingly treat me. It had been different with Linda, being a total stranger.

Jo had known about my 'marriage stand' – but after leaving her own husband, she made a bee-line for mine! Another diabolical 'set up' by satan. I was totally gutted – the terrible pain in my heart was all now too familiar, but now it felt much, much worse, as it involved a friend I thought I knew could be trusted. Apparently Pete, her husband, was just as devastated too. At this discovery, I declared out loud to the Lord: 'This time, Lord – I'm throwing in the towel on this "Standing-for-my-Marriage" lark.'

I said this as I was into my second bottle of wine, with a female neighbour friend of mine. I switched on my computer, only to find the very words I'd just used to the Lord were being quoted back at me by Charlyne Steinkamp of Rejoice Marriage Ministries on their daily email of encouragement, to the effect: 'If the devil is trying to cause you to "throw in the towel" on your stand for marriage – don't give up! The Lord is on your side'!

I've *never* sobered up so quickly as I did then – God means business.

Any readers getting thus far must think of saying to me, 'O for Heaven's sake, woman, aren't you normal like all of us? Why not give up now, and just move on? How can you forgive someone as close as that for stealing your own husband?'

Well, you might be interested and slightly relieved to hear that this time I found it excruciatingly painful – unbearable. It's hard when one has met and married the love of one's life, had a long history with one another together, and brought their children into the world, to give it all up, especially as this involved a 'friend'. But I knew if I needed *any* peace of mind, I had to trust God, and to try to forgive James and – now, Josephine.

~~

Forgiving was *in no way easy this time around* – in fact, I would go around like a bear with a sore head if *her* name was mentioned – which of course it was by my children who when little had looked upon her almost as a second mum. We'd spent so much time together as families. It took nine long months for me to reach that place of forgiveness; nine months in an already *annus horribilis* – lost earnings, rows with the kids, you name it. I also sustained a broken wrist, though the Lord provided me with the best neighbour ever, whose nursing skills came to the fore: she was marvellous. She helped me dress, cook, clean, eat, etc. It soon healed up, but by the end of September or early October, I was ill in bed – and felt like I was dying. This was just where the Lord wanted me, and that I should die – to *self*!

I had to go through the fiery furnace of dying to self. When self is on the throne, it's like the devil is sitting on my shoulder whispering his lies into my ears, preventing me from having a balanced view of either myself, others or the world. In the fiery furnace of God's extreme heat and love, these things get burned away. What's left is little – but it is the one thing the Lord can work with – a contrite and humble heart He will not despise (Psalm 51:17).

With God's help, and in my mind's eye, I was able to bring my husband and this 'friend' of mine to the Cross and leave them there for Him to deal with. Amazingly, not long after this confession and forgiveness, I learned from the children that James had *moved out* of Jo's home and had found a small place of his own about one hour's drive away from our home.

Humility and Spiritual Warfare

I began to humble myself before the Lord. I felt Him say that *I* needed to ask my husband for forgiveness for *my part* of the breakdown of the marriage – which I duly did, and which of course was music to his ears – but where would this lead us to?

For approximately three weekends, we would meet up for a chat and a drink, then James would back down and say that he wasn't ready yet – he needed more time. 'This word "time" again, Lord – how long this time?' was my lament. In my daily

Bible reading I felt I was told: *'Do not approach this people, but let them come to you – this time I will teach them my ways.'*

The church would say, 'God has given him free will; just let him be.' But, what they may not realise is that if one's free will is being overruled then one *cannot* think or act reasonably. As Jesus said to his Father whilst dying on the Cross ... 'Forgive them, Lord, *for they know not what they are doing*' [italics added]. It was time to practise the spiritual warfare that is suggested in the Scriptures: 'Finally brothers, be strong in the Lord and in the power of his might, putting on the whole armour of God, so that in the evil day we can stand ... etc. (Ephesians 6:10) It was time to apply the whole armour of God to ourselves and our loved ones. Also, Jesus said, 'What is bound on earth is bound in heaven, what is loosed on earth, is loosed in heaven' (Matthew 18:18). My husband was being deceived – so this spirit of deception needed binding from him, along with the enemy's evil tactics, so that divine deliverance could be loosed upon him. James's own free will was being violated. He needed to be released into everything that God had planned for him.

━━

CHAPTER THIRTY-NINE

CHILDHOOD MEMORIES

Courage, dear heart. (C. S. Lewis)

So much time went by whilst I was waiting for my miracle to happen. During this time, I received healing of a childhood memory. I was having a meal at a friend's house, and a lady there was telling them how the Lord had brought healing to her own childhood memory. This triggered a memory that I had, of when, at four years old, I went into hospital to have my tonsils out. Whenever I thought of that time, it was for me grey, lonely, scary and not very pleasant, but as I couldn't understand why, I thought now would be the time to ask the Lord to heal me of it – as that was what He had done for this other lady.

As I prayed, asking the Lord to 'restore to myself a sense of being', somehow, in the Spirit, the Lord took me back to being that four-year-old in hospital. It was visiting time and Jesus came and sat at my bedside and brought such light and colour into that grey drab place, then He smoothed my brow and kissed my forehead. Next, He was sitting on the other side of my bed (with me under the covers), then He was lying down and propped up on one elbow. He settled there to be alongside me – somewhere in the memory, I remember hearing a bell ringing to signify that visiting time was finishing – but Jesus said, no, He wasn't leaving. He said that He would *never* leave me or forsake me. He continued to show me the wounds in His hands and feet, head and back, and I cried and cried as He told me that He'd done this for me so I could be with Him and his Father forever and ever. I felt such peace as I looked into His kind and lovely eyes. He was praying to the Father that I would come to know Him one day. Jesus restored my heart and healed those memories. These were such soothing words of comfort and this applies to 'all who would believe' – doesn't that thrill your own soul to know He can do this?

Afterwards, I asked Mum about the hospital incident and immediately she remembered that, for some reason or other, she and my dad were unable to come and visit me – at least not as often as they had wished – and that she had felt guilty about that. I was able to tell her how Jesus had dealt with it, and to no longer feel guilty about it.

~~

My dear dad died in early 2004, and James did turn up for his funeral, which was a comfort. He came out of respect for my dad. Ben, Emily and I were greatly relieved to see him there – even despite there being little warmth between us.

October 2005 was our son's twenty-first birthday 'family' meal all together; the atmosphere was stormy. The photos of that event serves now to remind us of the clever masks we all wore to cover up our true feelings at the time – which were, no doubt, a sense of anger, frustration and the injustice of having our lovely family being torn apart by an unseen enemy, though not everyone really knew that. The Bible says that 'we are not dealing with flesh and blood, but principalities and powers in heavenly places' (Ephesians 6:12).

At the end of that month, I attended a Christian healing retreat, and shook out my 'spiritual dust bags' so to speak. There was much prayer and cutting off of previous, pre-Christian, deep and dingy relationship soul-ties etc. After being bathed in Christian prayers, I left that retreat feeling tons lighter and with my conscience and body cleansed.

By November, an email appeared in my inbox from James – he suggested we meet up ...

CHAPTER FORTY

THIRD RETURN, AND ….

*I can do things you cannot do, you can do things I cannot do. Together we can do
great things.* (Mother Teresa)

James and I met up for a walk. The stuffing was almost knocked out of me when
James informed me that, after a lot of thinking, he'd come to the conclusion and felt
that it was only right that *if* I agreed – that we be reunited and live under the same
roof. He knew that meant us *getting married again. Yes!*

By January 2006, at his suggestion, we met up with the pastor of my church. At
the end of April 2006, we first of all had a civil ceremony at the local Register Office
and then, a week later at my church in early May 2006, *we took our re-marriage vows*:
we were blessed before many, with our two, now-adult offspring looking on, a bit
bemused. The words which were given to me by the Lord, to be read out at our re-
marriage blessing ceremony, were from Ruth 1:16-17

> *… but Ruth replied, 'Don't urge me to leave you or to turn back from you. Where
> you go I will go, and where you stay I will stay. Your people will be my people and
> your God my God. Where you die I will die, and there I will be buried. May the
> LORD deal with me, be it ever so severely, if even death separates you and me.*

God is so good; true and faithful to His promises.

However, I was slightly unnerved when our Pastor's choice of sermon on the
occasion of our re-marriage, was from Hosea 2:14 & 15 "Therefore, behold I will
allure her and lead her to the wilderness, and speak to her tenderly. There I will give
back her vineyards and make the Valley of Achor (= Trouble) into a gateway of
hope…."

Hadn't we experienced enough trouble so far? Did this mean there was even
more to come?

Later, our daughter admitted that she doubted very much that this re-marriage would work out, seeing that although it was the 'right' thing to do both her Mum and Dad were still 'poles apart' in their beliefs and thinking. At that stage – and having developed a fascination with the land and its art and culture, Emily decided she would head to a country in 'the East' – in fact, almost as far as the East is from the West – to live and work, and ultimately – marry and settle.

⬛⬛

CHAPTER FORTY-ONE

SPIDER'S WEB

Man did not weave the web of life. He is merely a strand in it. Whatever he does to the web, he does to himself. (Chief Seattle)

The following Christmas, James asked what I would like from him. I asked whether we could have an old eternity diamond ring re-set, to look like a proper engagement ring. We had bought that diamond from South Africa, when James's brother worked there as a diamond broker, as an investment at the beginning of our first marriage. It had been set in a 'safe' setting, but not very exciting. Now, we took it to be re-modelled in the way I had in mind. Around the time of completion, I received a call from the jewellers: 'Mrs G – we apologise profusely, but your original diamond is now useless. It must have had a fault in it, as a piece had chipped off as the work was being done on it.'

As diamonds hardly ever break, they had *not* suggested insuring it beforehand. They were so apologetic: 'However, we promise to replace it – free of charge [God's grace] with a similar diamond.

James and I had to trust them to do so. The final specimen was just perfect. It seems there must be a parable somewhere in this diamond-ring story about our marriage. Another book maybe?

~~

We bought a narrow boat together and spent much time 'getting to know' one another again. We spent a couple of fun summer seasons exploring the canals around middle England. One morning, in my quiet time, I felt the Lord warn me that James wished to be soon rid of the narrow boat and would want to exchange it for something smaller and zippier. I quite enjoyed the gentle pace of our canal boat, but because I had been warned by the Lord, and much to James's surprise, I didn't overreact when he finally came out with his suggestion to exchange.

'I've been doing some thinking,' James said to me. 'I've had enough of this slow-paced boat. How about we sell it and buy something a bit faster – something with a bit of oomph?'

'That's OK with me,' came my reply, quite nonchalantly.

'Phew, I was convinced you'd be upset – seeing as you seem to enjoy the narrow boat. I must admit, I'm quite surprised – and relieved at your calm reaction,' said James.

Within a few months, that's exactly what happened. The canal boat was duly sold, and replaced by a smaller, much faster – from the sublime to the ridiculous – boat, which we kept on the south coast. James enjoyed taking this boat out – but I admit I didn't enjoy going out on it: I didn't feel safe on it at all.

There was one alarming incident that 'rocked my boat' so to speak. We were visiting James's sister and he had passed me his mobile phone to read an email that had come through for us both – when suddenly, whilst it was still in my hand – a text popped up from *Josephine* saying: 'Hey you – how's it going?' I was on the brink of tears and showed it to James. Though embarrassed about the incident, James quickly dismissed it and said it was nothing.

~~

All the while we were back together, I didn't speak about my faith – a miracle in itself – but there was an underlying tension between us. I had found an anniversary card to give to James depicting a spider dangling on a web – little did I know when I bought it, but that web representing our own marriage was getting thinner and thinner and more precarious. 'The spider' was hatching more trouble in the unseen places.

It was into our second year back together, when one evening James and I had a disagreement over some issue, the memory of which escapes me – but the resulting reactions that I then experienced way surpassed what would or should normally have happened. I just wept and wept uncontrollably for at least 40 minutes. It was as if, deep down in my spirit, I knew things between James and I were just not right.

Well, they weren't, as Emily had so rightly said; we were still poles apart, spiritually speaking. That spirit of temptation was lurking somewhere out in the shadows, waiting to pounce – and James was wobbling badly, knowing Josephine had been in touch. Notwithstanding my Christian commitment, which James thought he could manage, he still found it oppressive and limiting. Sundays were the worst, when there was a battle between my church time and James's desired leisure time. He found it all too much ...

━━

CHAPTER FORTY-TWO

THIRD BETRAYAL

"Resentment is like taking poison and waiting the other person to die"
Malachy McCourt

Luckily for James he's still alive!

'I see you have packed a Christmas present in the boot of the car – who is it for?' I asked James innocently. I knew he was going to make a quick visit to his sister's, but we had already organised her present.

He had poured himself a glass of wine and I asked him to pour me one also. He looked at me like the proverbial rabbit caught in the headlights.

'O *that?* – I, well, err I'm going to give it to – umm – Josephine.'

'Sorry, I don't think I heard you right? You mean, you *don't* actually mean, Jo ..., Jo ..., *Josephine*? I spat out her name.

'Y ... es.' And my husband confessed his continuing adultery with her.

'Whaaaaat?'

I was *so angry* that if I had had any sort of weapon to hand, I would have used it against him. The paltry wine glass just wasn't enough, though it smashed quite satisfactorily – *thwack* – as it hit him and shattered into hundreds of pieces on the floor, its contents spluttering over him and the wall behind. [I'm not the little doormat you mistook me for.]

'James, I don't *believe* what I'm hearing – this is *just not on*. How *could* you do this to me *again*?' I moaned – trying to appeal to him.

There was no response.

In the flash of the moment, I then understood how these unpremeditated 'crimes of passion' happen, almost involuntarily and totally unplanned. When you're 'seeing red' all reason goes out of the window.

Rather than hang around and do something I would regret afterwards, I grabbed my keys, handbag and coat, headed out of the door and got in my car ... driving, thinking ...

'Where? Where do I go?' Yes, to friends where I could cool off, simmer down and spend the night. (At a later stage, I received ministry for that anger – it's an all-too-powerful emotion.)

I just *knew* things weren't right – and I was correct. It emerged that Josephine, alas, never did get out from under James's skin; this happened just two days before Christmas 2008.

Meanwhile, when waking up at the house of my friends, I found myself singing the chorus to another Graham Kendrick song, in which the words went 'For this I have Jesus. For this I have Jesus' Yes, thankfully, for *all* I was going through, I still had my Jesus.

Upon my return to the flat, James had packed some belongings and had gone – again. Oh, this zig-zag of emotions. I felt compelled to write to Jo telling her in no uncertain terms, 'What God has joined together, let *no one* separate' (Matthew 19:6), and that I 'wouldn't wish the consequences of that upon my worst enemy – *let alone* my friend.'

CHAPTER FORTY-THREE

HELLO, SQUARE ONE

Anything can happen if you let it. (Mary Poppins)

Despite circumstances looking the absolute opposite of favourable, I found my consolation in Christ. In His strength alone was I able to forgive James and Josephine. Amazingly, I still believed the Lord for James's and my reconciliation and for my husband's salvation. Jesus continued to be my *faithful husband and Lord*. I found the words from the book of Ruth so comforting: 'The LORD, the God of Israel, under whose wings you have come to take refuge' (Ruth 2:12).

The Lord's Business

In the September of that year, I heard that James's sister, who had been seriously ill, had just been moved to a hospice within an hour's journey of my home. My Bible readings one morning in particular were prompting me: *'You must speak my words to them, whether they listen or fail to listen, for they are rebellious.'* I started remonstrating to the Lord: 'But Lord, James's family don't even *like* me.' Then, when my computer broke down and I was unable to finish my work that day, I *knew* God meant business. So, trusting the Lord for the right moment to speak to her, I drove to pay a visit to my dear sister-in-law. She was asleep when I arrived. I reminded the Lord that if He wished me to speak to her, then He must wake her up soon, before other visitors arrived. She then opened her eyes and smiled to see me there. That was a relief. I had just been able to say, 'And *anyone* who calls on the Name of the Lord, will be saved,' when in walked her older sister, asking me what *I* was doing there. The sick sister died a few days later. Although I didn't attend the funeral, Emily and Ben reported that it was very peaceful, though sad, but 'with a nice atmosphere'. I thanked God that I hadn't refused His promptings that day, as I felt sure my late sister-in-law must have made her peace with the Lord and is with Him now in heaven.

I have since made my peace with James's remaining sister.

~~

My lovely mum died in early September 2010, and my estranged husband James came, again out of respect, to her funeral. My vast family had little idea what had taken place between James and me, so they all received him well. And for a short time, all 'seemed to be well'.

CHAPTER FORTY-FOUR

LUMPS AND BUMPS

"Fasten your seat belts – it's going to be a bumpy night" Bette Midler

Around November 2010, James came to help me with some odd jobs needed in my flat. After our re-marriage, we had sold the cottage-type house and moved into a flat within a couple of miles. The ubiquitous James had bought a flat in London, where he was now working for a London-based recruitment firm, and living – on his own.

'How come all my clothes are still in the cupboard, just as I had left them?' he asked.

'Well, they're yours and they're waiting for you,' came my response. There seemed to be a long pause.

'I've just been offered a job in the Middle East,' James proffered. 'How would you feel if I took up the job in the Middle East and I asked *you* to join me?'

After reading *all* of the above sordid details of this narrative, you might have thought my obvious answer to him would have been, *'No way!'* but, as I was still married to him, and with us having so much history, I was able to brush off the cobwebs of the many promises that the Lord had given me. So, I agreed that, *if* he was to go (which he did), then I would come out to join him – initially for a holiday. I booked to spend Easter 2011 with him but, in the month of February, I discovered a lump on my right breast ...

~~

One particular morning, before going to my work with a charity – which involved taking married couples into schools for dialogues with young people on marriage and relationships – I had assessed my breast in the shower and thought, 'This is more like a mass than a lump and it looks like it's puckering ...'

Well, again, my Lord was one step ahead of the game. After the particular couple at the school event that day had answered the students' questions about their marriage of fifty-four years – during which time the wife had experienced breast cancer – the husband stood up and said:

'Ladies,' – there was only a group of Year 10 students, and myself – 'when my wife had this problem, *she didn't actually find a lump - it was more like a mass, and it looked like it was puckering.*'

'OK, Lord. You have my attention now,' I said under my breath.

I made an appointment with the doctor, who confirmed it was a stage 2 cancerous lump, though, interestingly, it didn't show on a mammogram. But I insisted on having a scan. I said to the consultant, at the unwelcome news: 'Well, thanks be to God – at least I have *Him* in my life, and I choose not to be afraid, and trust in Him for my healing.'

'Well, yes. Er... mmm, of course, Mrs G. Very good, that's alright for *you*,' came the reply.

In no time at all, I was sent to hospital, and had a successful lumpectomy, followed by daily radiotherapy for three weeks. I was surrounded by much care from friends and hospital staff. This strange and unwelcome change of routine of my life was indeed a real eye-opener. Every day I would either be driven by friends or just go by myself to the radiotherapy department of the local hospital. I felt I was one of the lucky ones. There were others – mostly bald as a result of having undergone chemotherapy and who were now having radiotherapy – looking gaunt and terrified. I was able to share my faith with a few, as I was given a supernatural amount of peace during that time.

It was the time of the tsunami in Japan, and I was watching footage on the BBC News website. A camera was facing towards the sea, showing a fishing boat. Suddenly the *gigantic* wave rose up like a monster in front, but the boat just seemed to ride the wave, without toppling. In my spirit, I felt the Lord say: *'I am with you in this trial, you won't topple.'* Praise God, it's more than eight years on and I am still cancer-free. Having the 'C' word in my life did at times make me tremble with fear – and there were nights when I'd toss and turn asking the 'Why me?' question. Was I being 'punished and judged' for my previously sinful life? These suggestions were of the devil; the truth is that Jesus was judged for me and bore my punishment on the Cross. I would text a friend, knowing she would be up late and I would voice my fears. As if by magic, a text would come pinging back quoting something from God's word, which would have such a calming effect on me that I would turn over and sleep like a baby. The truth of God's word is so healing.

~~

At this stage James came over from abroad to 'look after me'. He was also involved in the radiotherapy rota of taking me for treatment. It was a few months later that I joined him where he was now living, in the sun, for a very welcome month of recuperation. Emily and Ben were able to join us for the first ten days and we were a family once more – taking up (again) where we had left off – only now our children were maturing into adults. We had mad games in the swimming pool and enjoyed picnics down on the beach. I can't remember quite how it happened but we were all running into the sea, and I managed to fall headlong, flat on my face, before even reaching the water.

'Oh, Mother! What a sight you are,' screamed Emily and Ben with laughter as I brushed the little pebbles, sand and seaweed out of my hair and teeth.

Whilst there, James and I discussed the possibility of my coming over to join him on a more permanent basis. So, I returned to the UK and handed in my notice to my job, where fortunately a successful incumbent was soon found to replace me.

However, by mid-October an alarming email appeared in my inbox from James. He had had a change of mind about our previously discussed arrangements and requested that *I didn't join him* in the new year.

'Why?'

Even more *heartbreak*. This was a very *black* time indeed. I also realised that Josephine was still hovering in the background somewhere.

━━

CHAPTER FORTY-FIVE

FURNACE

Disappointments are just God's way of saying, 'I've got something better – Be patient ... Live life ... Have faith. (Lanette Sem)

I found I was for three, possibly four, months in the midst of wallowing in the pit of self-pity – *not* a good place to be – and in the furnace of unforgiveness and a very real place called 'Disappointment'. I felt like a locomotive shunted down a siding: my spiritual life was dry, grey and lifeless – the joy of the Lord definitely in short supply. Having attended the 'university of hard knocks' for too many terms of my life, it slowly dawned on me that there were two people in my life towards whom I was feeling bitter and unloving, and although I *thought* I had forgiven them seventy times seven times – or whatever the biblical mathematics was – I realised that I had only accomplished that with my head and *not* my heart. Now it was time to get back on track with the Lord.

My Bible opened at Isaiah 60:15: 'Although you have been forsaken and hated, with no one traveling through, I will make you the everlasting pride and the joy of all generations.' And although this was a message to Israel, it felt very pertinent to my current situation so, once again, I welcomed this comforting word from the Lord. The amount of perseverance and tenacity I was given was just unbelievable. The Bible says, 'When we are weak, He makes us strong' (2 Corinthians 12:9).

It's only at the Cross that we can discover true forgiveness – the place where that glorious exchange took place: *His* Righteousness for *our* sin. I was shown again in no uncertain terms those words of Jesus from John 20:22-23 when, after His resurrection, and appearing to the disciples in the upper room, Jesus breathed on them and said: 'Receive the Holy Spirit. *If you forgive anyone's sins, their sins are forgiven; if you do not forgive them, they are not forgiven.*' Then, of course, the Lord's Prayer (Luke 11:4): ... *Forgive us our sins, for we also forgive everyone who sins against us* ...and finally Matthew 18:21-35 tells the story of the unforgiving debtor – about *forgiving from the heart* (italics added).

I knew I was being held in torment – so I repented of my own hardened heart and asked for God's mercy. After reading a book about this very topic, I realised I wanted to be one who blesses and not curses, one who forgives and not one who judges or holds on to grudges.

'It is mine to avenge,' says the Lord – so with God's gracious help, I once more brought these two individuals, in my mind's eye, to the foot of the Cross, and released them to Him; I told the Lord: 'I'm willing to forgive them – because of your blood shed for *me*.' And with that I entrusted them into His hands *for Him* to deal with – again. No longer could those invisible binds that I had spun around them with unforgiveness prevent God from reaching these ones, for as I released them to Him, so the weight of my hardened heart just melted away – only to be replaced by His glorious peace.

I even felt able to pray *a blessing* upon them! Whether these individuals deserved to be forgiven or not, I knew *that I* had to obey His command to forgive, and trust *Him* to sort them out, because I certainly could not. For me, it felt so good to be back on the receiving end of His forgiveness for my 'holding back forgiveness' to others – having learned once more to 'return to the Cross of Christ'. Yes, it was definitely a great place to reside and abide in peace and joy, knowing *my* sins are forgiven. Thanks be to God.

⬤⬤

CHAPTER FORTY-SIX

THIRD ISHMAEL?

Keep the faith – the most amazing things in life tend to happen right at the moment you're about to give up hope. (Prakhar Sahay)

Something happened in 2012 that James hadn't banked on: our daughter announced her engagement to her boyfriend. They returned to the UK from the East, as did James, for their marriage in the autumn of that year. The day was perfect from beginning to end. The sun shone, the happy couple laughed their way through most of the ceremony and on into the afternoon and evening. So, once again the Gaults were able to play 'happy families' during the time of our daughter and her husband's nuptials. Following one of the most wonderfully blessed and happiest days of my life; their wedding, I was ready to take a holiday in the sun. James suggested I join him for two weeks, which again surprisingly, I agreed to. I had been told that Josephine was 'no longer on the scene'. Funnily enough, I had received the same Bible reading from Ruth 1:16 both the day before arriving (i.e. 'where you go, I'll go' etc.) and the day I left. I wish I had prayed through that one beforehand. I realised then that *you can't assume anything with the Lord*. Things 'seemed' to go well between James and me.

Over supper one night before my return to the UK, James surprised me by saying: 'What you have found, i.e. Christianity, is good – I just wish *I* could find it too.' (That sounded familiar somehow.) But so shocked was I that I didn't actually respond, but excused myself and went into the bathroom, got down on my knees and gave thanks to the Lord.

For the first time *ever* I allowed myself a tiny glimpse of that light at the end of the tunnel. The Lord gave me permission 'to dream' again.

The Lord's Waiting Room

I had been praying for and awaiting a breakthrough for years; it was as if I had

had an appointment at the doctor's office and I was kept waiting and waiting for my name to be called, but nothing seemed to be happening. Others were called in, but I was kept there waiting for what seemed like a long, long time. The Lord alone has enabled me to persevere and kept me strong, standing firm.

Now, it was if He was saying to me: *'Daughter, the end of the race is within sight now and you will go through that finishing line. I am going to make the crooked path straight for you ...'*

But before that crooked path was made straight ....

‒‒

CHAPTER FORTY-SEVEN

A GAME OF THRONES

Be a pineapple: stand tall, wear a crown, and be sweet on the inside. (Unknown)

James had booked to come back to the UK to spend Christmas with Ben and me. Or so I had thought. *Wrong* again; hopes dashed. This all seemed like horribly familiar territory.

Ben and I had just finished making some mulled wine, the festive aroma of which pervaded the whole flat. We had strung a few Christmas cards up and decorated the now much-smaller tree, when Ben received a call from his dad, with words to the effect: 'Sorry old chap – but won't be with you this Christmas – hope you understand. However, a 'family meal' has been arranged on New Year's Day and so if you'd like to attend, I shall arrange to pick you up from the train station. Merry Christmas. Bye for now.'

So although he came back – it was, alas, not to us. Yep, you guessed right – look at *the* time of year. The fight continued to rage in my husband's mind – and such a battle for souls was going on, amidst the greatest one, for marriage and families; much praying was needed.

Sadness, disappointment and more heartache were poised to pounce once more upon my heart. But the Lord came to my rescue. He sent a friend. She was given a 'picture' from Him – it was almost like I was seated on a huge overstuffed chair – it looked more like a throne.

Although the evil one wanted to put Josephine there – in my place – at the 'family meal', God, who is on *the throne* had much bigger ideas, and no usurper was going to push me out permanently. The Bible says, 'we are seated with Him in the heavenly places' (Ephesians 2:6) – and so, He was saying that *no one* could take my place.

This filled my heart with hope and a joy that no man could take away.

Earlier in the year, this same friend, the one who had helped me when I had broken my wrist, had been given a 'picture' of James: he was the Lord's 'trophy' – this trophy had been covered in sludge and was being hauled out of a deep dark stinking pit. God hosed him down and cleaned him up. She was shown the stunning shining end result – a trophy of *pure* gold. Psalm 40:2 says: 'He lifted me out of the slimy pit, out of the mud and mire; He set my feet on a rock and gave me a firm place to stand.'

~~

Apparently this 'coming and going' of stops and false starts is quite common amongst returning prodigals. With conflicting voices in their ears, it's no wonder there's so much confusion.

A returned prodigal – the late Bob Steinkampf – once wrote: 'Your prodigal makes false starts toward home or toward family events and then just as suddenly withdraws or backs out.'

Was this not my husband's experience to a 'T'?

CHAPTER FORTY-EIGHT

IDOLS

Forget what hurt you, but never forget what it taught you. (Shannon L. Alder)

We need to rewind back to November 2011, where, at a conference in the southwest of England, I was given a prophecy. The lady who gave it to me said: 'Like Abraham, you need to take your Isaac up the mountain and place him on the altar for sacrifice – but the Lord will provide a ram' (the story can be found in Genesis 22).

At the time, I wasn't quite sure what she meant but *by now* I had learned that *James* had become 'my idol' – and the Lord will not accept *any* idols before him. I must worship God alone. So, in my mind's eye, I fully placed James on the Lord's altar and said to Him: 'There's *nothing* I can do for James, except pray – so I hand him over to you for you to deal with. He's all yours.' The Lord had most probably been waiting for me to do this *for a long time* – I confess to being a slow learner at times – or more to the point, just plain stubborn.

So, it was time to forgive again – not only James and Jo, but this time myself. I received a lot of encouragement from other Christian friends over this time. Once again, my heart was spared more pain, and it seemed the Lord was really ministering to me.

~~

We would all love to say that we got things right all the time, wouldn't we? But there's no such thing as perfection here on earth – alas, I felt I failed miserably so often. But, Jesus is my Advocate. I have learned again and again to lean on and trust in the Lord and His faithfulness alone and certainly not be so flippant about the importance of forgiveness. I also find I'm being more empathetic to those living on their own – not by their own choice. I soon realised, to the Christian, Christ is 'our everything'; often I tried 'flying solo' and thought that I could operate perfectly well without his love and guidance – but that's absolutely futile. I would fall flat on my face every time. Mercifully, He is there to pick me up, brush me down and set me back on track again and again. He will do this for anyone who trusts in Him.

Dream

In the mid-summer of 2013, I had a dream whilst staying at a friend's house: James and I were at a small table in a restaurant. He was very attentive towards me and kept leaning over as if wanting to kiss me.

Later on that day, a lovely man of God – friend of my friend – confirmed that the dream was from the Lord. Wow, God so often has 'dropped these treasures into my darkness' – He is *so good*.

On the 1st January 2014, I definitely felt a new excitement in my spirit. I felt the Lord say: *'Behold, I am doing a new thing – the old has gone and the new has come. Fear not for I am with you. Things are happening that you cannot see right now, but you need to prepare your heart and your life* (cf. Isaiah 43:18-19). *For my promises are about to be fulfilled – for I am the faithful One – so unchanging.'*

Three months into that year, 'the thaw' as mentioned in my Parable of the Freezer, finally was beginning to take place.

Another Dream

I went to bed one night, with Josephine on my mind – I was still praying blessings over her. That night I dreamt that I bumped into Jo. We were in a park and Jo was sitting on a bench with an older couple (maybe her parents?). Anyhow, I called her name, went up to her in my dream and embraced her. Then I awoke with such *peace*, knowing that *this time* I had truly forgiven her. James had informed and assured me – and I believed him this time – that 'it was finally *all over* with Josephine'.

~~

So, you have every right to ask: 'Why do you believe this man *this* time? What's different?'

CHAPTER FORTY-NINE

GOOD NEWS – THE GOSPEL

... for it is by grace you have been saved, through faith – and this is not from yourself, it is the gift of God ... (Ephesians 2:8)

James had three years living on his own on the island in the sun and, towards the end of 2013 and at the beginning of 2014, he came to the conclusion that unless he changed, his life was going to be pretty bleak. It happened that at that time, having just returned to where he was staying abroad from the UK, one Sunday evening in that January, James googled 'Alpha Course' in that town. To his amazement he discovered that there was a course starting not more than two miles from him on the following Tuesday evening. Subsequently, James went each Tuesday to the New Testament Church meeting hall. He did not find it easy and on occasions wanted to quit. At the end of the ten-week course there was the Holy Spirit weekend, and this James thought would be 'it' – he would finally find God. Regrettably, and despite the minister's attempt to induce the Holy Spirit in him by giving James enormous and embarrassing bear hugs, nothing happened. Needless to say, he was more than dispirited and quite frankly at a pretty low point.

... But God

Nevertheless, a week later James found himself back in the New Testament Church, when a Jonathan Conrathe from Mission 24 spoke, and James found his message of Jesus, redemption, forgiveness and salvation to be utterly compelling. It was, as they say, as if God was talking directly to him – and James found Jonathan's invitation to meet Jesus irresistible. Although over the ensuing few years, James has doubted this experience, the fact is that *it happened* and James believes that Jesus exists and that he, James, is saved and forgiven.

~~

I also had reason to believe that God was working on 'the other side of the mountain' in my prodigal husband's life: he had been emailing me with question after question on the Christian faith. James told me that he had sought out and had attended this same Alpha Course and, in his communications to me, he admitted that he had finally come to 'the end of himself'.

This time, his words were *very* loving, and there were *many* times he asked forgiveness for all the ways he had treated me – in a genuinely repentant tone. He knew that he needed to make the right decision for his life as he finally realised *right* from *wrong*, i.e. he admitted he had been living 'in deception'. I could hardly believe what my ears were hearing.

All the shattering of my heart and mind which I had experienced over the past 15 years or so, all the devastation that had previously taken place, was all beginning to be smoothed over by the balm of God's promises being fulfilled, and the actual witness of seeing my husband's attitude change so drastically. God had taken those tiny fragments and had indeed built them up *His way* and he was now preparing something beautiful to behold. I was in total awe of what my Lord was up to. I could hardly contain my excitement.

This was when the quote from Isaiah 43:19 began to mean very much to me – that He would 'make a way in the wilderness and send streams in the desert ...'

━━

CHAPTER FIFTY

BEST NEWS OF ALL!

Sing like no one is listening, love like you've never been hurt, dance like nobody is watching, and live like it's Heaven on Earth. (Mark Twain)

The best news of all – for me, at least – was that James had become a Christian. He had explained that it was *not* on the Alpha Course, but the following week, when the Lord had sent a British evangelist to the place where James was living, to the actual church he was attending. At the altar call, James felt compelled to go forward and respond. He experienced a very personal, tailor-made encounter with the Lord, which left him in no doubt that He, Jesus, is *alive* – and that all James's sins were forgiven.

Things then really started to accelerate and James was practically on the next flight home to discuss our future. My first reaction was to dance around my flat giving thanks and singing praises to my faithful God and Saviour at the *top of my voice*. I then sent up a prayer to the Lord: 'Please let James wish to meet up with the pastor of my church', who had blessed our re-marriage almost eight years earlier. And would you know it, the day he arrived, over a bowl of soup and a drink at a local pub, James asked me for my pastor's contact details. They arranged to meet up and I was invited to join them after a full hour had passed.

Pastor J. assured me: 'This is a different James than the one I reluctantly re-married to you back in 2006. Would you like to take your marriage vows once more – but this time more meaningfully and to the Lord to whom *you both* now belong?' And *so we did* – there and then in his office! This time it was quite surreal. No hats, suits, wedding dresses or confetti; no bells and smells – just the pastor, with James and me repeating those same vows we had taken almost eight years earlier – and, originally, 37 years earlier. But there was a joy, a lightness, plus a sense of *awe*, which was definitely missing at either of our two previous exchanges of vows. The Lord was in our midst.

With reference to the verses from Hosea, which I had previously found unnerving – I was indeed 'lured back into the desert/wilderness', where the Lord spoke tenderly to my heart, during those times of further trouble. I felt so comforted to read the words from Song of Songs Chapter 7 verse 5 – "Who is this coming up from the wilderness leaning on her Beloved?" It all takes time; it's a process this faith-walk. None of us know the tailor-made path the Lord has planned for each one of His children, but with His help and perseverance, we will surely get there. We all as Christians need to reach that point in our walk with Him, to be able to surrender it ALL to Him – it then becomes as pleasurable as "skiing on oil!"

~~

Very shortly before our reunion, the evil one *tried* using two very trusted friends of mine, who both independently came up to me and said that I had every right to 'let James go, permanently, and not bother with him anymore – and just get on with your life'. Fortunately, as I confided this to another dear friend, who had understood exactly the meaning of my 'marriage stand', prayed for me to have both wisdom and discernment as she believed God was about to do 'something *big*'. See how that cruel enemy muscles his way in to try to prevent God's will being done? Of course, I forgave my misguided friends; they were able to rejoice over the reconciliation between James and me.

~~

James returned abroad briefly to sort out his business affairs and then moved back permanently to the UK. Together we sold our flat – at the first offer – and have since moved away from that area to another more rural area in the southwest of England. The Lord had gone ahead of us and had prepared just the right property for us.

==

CHAPTER FIFTY-ONE

A GODLY INHERITANCE

... till death us do part ... (Church of England Marriage Vows)

For the first few weeks after we moved in – James and I had ear-to-ear grins – we were once again like 'babes in the wood', only this time in our mid-sixties, but giving thanks to the Father for His wonderful miracle of another chance at being married to each other again, and for the amazing provision of such a beautiful property. All our furniture fitted exactly – the family table taking pride of position. The only extra cost was for curtains and blinds, and the odd fitted wardrobe. Having moved in early autumn, it wasn't until the following summer that we came to realise how much fruit grew in abundance in our new garden. I see this as a prophetic picture, of all the 'seeds' that have been sown into our marriage and those of future generations – which, we trust, will bear much fruit for God's kingdom.

All the heartache, the tears, the stops and starts, the hopelessness, all the refining process, the humbling, the 'not giving up when things looked bleak', all the pain we had gone through – we could honestly say that it was worth it all. Despite the odds being stacked up against us, the Lord is rebuilding us brick by brick, making firm our foundations. He is faithful to all His promises.

James and I are now embarking on whatever the journey is that the Lord has long been preparing. He is already fulfilling a promise (from Joel 2:25) that He would 'make up for all the years that the locusts have eaten ...'

As you can imagine, not everyone jumped for joy at our reunion. In particular our offspring were, naturally, wary of all that was going on. However, our daughter being married herself now for a few years, warmed to the idea of having her parents back together, and accepted it gladly. And with the arrival of our first grandchild, plus another one on the way, this reconciliation makes it all the more special. These grandchildren will grow up and possibly learn one day of the story of their grandparents' troubled marriage and eventual reconciliation. Hopefully they will be thankful that they neither gave up on each other nor stayed apart for ever.

Back in Emily's university days – so convinced was I at the time that it was only her dad who needed forgiveness – my own eyes were then blinded to the part I had played in the breakdown of our marriage. Once I acknowledged this, Emily was able to forgive me and we made up our differences. Only very recently have I been able to fully grasp how my behaviour then must have deeply affected our children. This understanding was triggered when there was a recent sermon at church being preached on Joseph and his brothers – finally forgiving each other for all their misdemeanours (found in Genesis 50:15-21). The obnoxious young Joseph needed as much to be forgiven by his brothers, as did Joseph need to forgive his brothers for their ill treatment of him. Thankfully, by that time, Joseph had come to realise the Lord's great love, and the power of forgiveness – and that 'in all things God works for the good of those who love Him' (Romans 8:28). It was like a light being switched on in my spirit. It gave me a helpful overview of our circumstances, as this story from the Old Testament so echoed our experience; the being disciplined over time and the consequences of forgiveness.

Ben, though very sceptical at first, understandably, came around to the idea of his parents being a permanent item. He and his fiancée were married just two years ago – with a beautiful summer wedding – where, as you can imagine, a *whole* family being gathered together once more was indeed a very special memorable time. They too are expecting a little one in the new year. Its so wonderful that James and I together can rejoice in becoming grandparents.

Both Ben and Emily are probably relieved to have 'Mum off their hands'. James and I are thankful that despite all that we had put our offspring through, they are still *pro*-marriage, thanks be to God. It could so easily have gone the other way. In His timing, the Lord will heal *their* broken hearts also. And my prayer would be, having put a stake in the ground for our own marriage, that this will help protect all future generations' marriages and that these marriages will truly last 'till death do them part' – that theirs would be a godly inheritance, indeed. Amen.

==

CHAPTER FIFTY-TWO

WHY DOES GOD HATE DIVORCE?

Divorce is like when you get Super Glue stuck on your fingers – you tear the flesh, whilst trying to tear them apart. (Rev. Greg Haslam)

I had heard this quote from my then pastor, Greg Haslam, long before our divorce. Following our divorce and before our reconciliation, I can now agree that it was the most painful thing I had *ever* experienced.

A quote from the New Testament: 'Therefore a man shall leave his father and mother and hold fast to his wife, and the two shall become one flesh' – is Paul writing to the Ephesians (5:31), and he continues … 'this mystery is profound, and I am saying that it refers to Christ and the church' (5:32). It's an indication of Christ's permanent love for his bride (the Church). Marriage was God's idea in the first place. It's not a contract to be entered into lightly, as has been previously mentioned, but it's a covenant with God – to be entered into when two parties agree.

Yes, God hates divorce; He hates what it does to people as a consequence, but He still *loves the people* who divorce. When it occurs, He knows the pain, the shame, the condemnation and all the connotations of divorce which affects His bride – and hence the surrounding society and the children in particular. Jesus says that the evil one comes only to steal, kill and destroy (John 10:10) but that He, Jesus, came to bring us life – life in all its fullness. In His great love for each of us, it was never intended that we should 'fall out of love' with Him, or with our spouses.

Psalm 103:14 says, 'The LORD knows our frame; He is mindful that we are dust.' Through Moses, He allowed divorce because of the hardness of men's hearts – but it was never meant to be that way.

Despite my own initial feelings of 'self-righteousness'; my determination to 'save' my marriage; it was through God's grace *alone* that I was able to pursue and continue to make a stand for my marriage. Whilst going through divorce, concurrently a friend was having marital problems – the full extent of which I had never understood at the time. As a result, I would legalistically lambast her with 'biblical truths' – insisting she should hang in there for the sake of her marriage etc., only to discover that what the Lord had spoken to *her*, was very different to what He had spoken to *me*. I believe the Lord had spoken clearly to me what His will was for *our* marriage, but for others, including the likes of this godly friend, it was a totally different outcome, as He speaks to us in different ways. Only He knows what is best for each of our individual circumstances. He will never contradict His word because He is the omnipotent, omniscient and omnipresent Lord.

I was extremely grateful for this lesson in God's grace, as it saved a very valued relationship between me and that friend. There's no doubt that the complex issues which surround divorce cause misunderstandings, bad feelings and divided loyalties which can result in a total fall-out of friendship within family and friendship circles – another reason possibly why God hates divorce.

~~

At this stage I would like to humble myself before God, my husband James, our now-adult children and any family or friends I've upset in the past, and ask for their forgiveness for my great lack of subtlety, wisdom and sensitivity in the early years of my Christian walk – which all added to the melange of what then took place in all of our lives. Thankfully we serve a God who literally 'wipes the slate clean'.

CHAPTER FIFTY-THREE

FIVE YEARS ON

Never give up praying for someone who seems to have a heart as hard as a rock.
One little seed (The Word of God) can reach the hardest heart, and soften it and bring
forth rich and fruitful branches that will glorify God! (Crusita Ollervides Sosa)

I have just asked my beloved how the last five years have been for him. His reply: 'I wouldn't change a thing.'

And the feeling is mutual. We are now becoming the married couple we were meant to be in the first place. Just a slight learning curve, you could say! The Lord thankfully is at the centre of this marriage – well, let's say we are working on it. It's 'baby steps' all the way – but James is letting the word of God shape his thoughts and attitudes bit by bit, whilst I need to display much understanding and patience.

I cannot be his teacher, and don't wish to be, but already I see such thrilling changes in him on a daily basis – the fruits of the Spirit are very evident: love, joy, peace, patience, kindness, faithfulness, gentleness and self-control (Galatians 5:22). Of course, I have much to put into practice by keeping my lips zipped and allowing James to take his place as the rightful 'head of this household'. What was acutely missing in our past 'marriages' was the earnest care for one another and the laughter that James and I now enjoy, as we can see the funny side of life together. We joke and giggle like little kids at times.

In the November of our first year back together, there was a visiting preacher to the tiny off-the-beaten-track church that we attended and, at the end of the service, he came towards James and me with the following words: 'The Lord is calling you and anointing you to do something new.' It was a great confirmation to know that we are in the Lord's will for our lives.

The sort of work that I used to do, albeit on a voluntary basis now, involved taking married couples into schools for dialogues about their marriages. Now, instead of wearing the 'facilitator's hat' it is in the capacity of a visiting 'married couple' that James and I occasionally participate. With so many marriages falling apart and the outlook looking bleak for these young people's future – we are able to encourage them by bringing them *hope*. Though our story might sound very extreme, and there were many questions on how *trust* could ever be built up after so many let-downs, all I could respond was that if it's the Lord's doing: then its *Him* I'm trusting in to finish the work that He started in James and myself. Isaiah 2:22 says, 'Don't put your trust in mere humans ...'

Psalm 127:1 says: 'Unless the LORD builds the house, the builders labour in vain. So it would be folly to ignore those words, for James and me at least. I know this stand for marriage is a life-long commitment. God's love is the only thing that has kept me sane on this long journey. He kept me in His firm grip. My God is faithful and His love knows no bounds, and He is always there to give us grace and mercy. And, as the English Poet Francis Thompson coined the phrase that the Lord is 'The Hound of Heaven', He never gave up on chasing James to the point of final submission.

The verses from Isaiah 61:3b-4 recently caught my attention. They say: 'They will be called oaks of righteousness, a planting of the LORD for the display of his splendour. They will rebuild the ancient ruins and restore the places long devastated; they will renew the ruined cities that have been devastated for generations.' This, I believe, is part of our remit for the future.

May his presence go with us wherever we go and wherever he sends us, and may *many* people be blessed as a result of hearing or reading this story! This is far from being a literary masterpiece and I have written it just as I speak, but I am trusting that the 'whosoevers' out there who might read this, will be able to resonate with what's been written, and might be able to correct the trajectory of *their own* journeys; so that they too are able to know the joy of reconciliation and marriage restoration. I feel like doing cartwheels with joy over all that the Lord has done and is doing for us. It would indeed be wonderful if just *one* marriage (hopefully more) might be saved from destruction after being encouraged by this tale of trials, tribulations and, finally, triumph.

As the Lord had previously said – His plans are certainly coming about in ways we could *never* have thought of or imagined! We are now looking forward to 'growing old together' as was originally promised. There's no guarantee of an easy ride, but it's faith that pleases Him, and oils the wheels on the journey.

Thank you, Lord. All Your promises are 'Yes' and 'Amen' in Christ Jesus
(2 Corinthians 1:20).
All the glory goes to God, the God and Father of our Lord Jesus Christ. Thank You, Lord!
WE GIVE YOU PRAISE; WE GIVE YOU GLORY; WE GIVE YOU ALL THE HONOUR.

CHAPTER FIFTY-FOUR

JAMES

On reflection and without doubt, I am extremely glad that I was 'sent' away from the UK. I felt God had said: 'Enough is enough.'

I needed time on my own; without any pressure to be free to pursue my faith independently.

I also at this stage wish to offer an abject apology – specifically to Patricia my wife, our two adult children, and to family and close friends. I like to think that our life on earth is a schooling for another life. At school one makes mistakes …

This really completes the account. Patricia and I are now reunited permanently; I am back where I belong, and we are very happy. Also, we are able to share a faith and live in harmony and compatibility. I am enormously grateful for the patience that she (and our children) have shown over the years and am humbled by their forgiveness.

━━

CHAPTER FIFTY-FIVE

JAMES AND PATRICIA

We would say to anyone going through painful times of deep betrayal of trust, with no seeming hope of the situation changing for the better – to truthfully call on the Lord in your time of need or trouble. He will give you that hope you crave. He strains to hear your voice calling out to Him. You are so precious to Him. He is no respecter of people – He has no favourites. He loves you with an everlasting and unconditional love. His love never fails. His love is 'stronger than death itself' (from Song of Songs).

If He has done this for *us* – then He *will* surely do it for *you*.

God's love never fails, Love always wins!